BUGS THAT LOVE!

The Amazing Western Conifer Seed Bug (& Shield Bugs Too!)

BY LORI-MICHELE

BUGS THAT LOVE!
The Amazing Western Conifer Seed Bug (& Shield Bugs Too!)
By Lori-Michele

Text copyright © 2020 by Lori-Michele
Illustrations copyright © 2020 by Lori-Michele
Hand lettering copyright © 2020 by Lori-Michele
All photographs copyright © 2020 by Lori-Michele

ALL RIGHTS RESERVED
No part of this book may be reproduced, or transmitted in any form or by any means, electronic or mechanical, including photocopying, recording, scanning or otherwise or by any information storage and retrieval system, without express written permission from the publisher.

Library of Congress Control Number: 2020916017
ISBN 978-0-9846172-5-8

Publisher- Lori-Michele
         Newfield, NY

Cover and back cover illustrated by Lori-Michele
 © 2020 by Lori-Michele

Legal & Medical Disclaimer: Use of the advice and information contained in this book are at the sole choice and risk of the reader. The author and publisher shall have neither liability nor responsibility to any person or entity with respect to any of the information contained in this book. The user assumes all risk for any injury, loss or damage caused or alleged to be caused, directly or indirectly by using any information in this book.

*Please make sure not to misidentify bugs, especially when handling them.

DEDICATION

To my father, for giving me his opinion and advice when I needed it and helping me with those certain key words, when I just didn't know how to sum it up.

And to both my mother & father, for showing and teaching me to have an appreciation and love for all things in nature.

"You'd be surprised to know, just how much these bugs can love!"

Lori-Michele

"BUGS THAT LOVE! is a fascinating book for young and old alike. Lori-Michele has spent 11 years watching and learning amazing and endearing qualities about the Western Conifer Seed Bug and Shield Bugs. Children will quickly realize that there is more to insects than they ever imagined. For one thing, they have distinct personalities. Read the book to find out how much more."

Dr. Jane Goodall, DBE,
Founder of the Jane Goodall Institute &
UN Messenger of Peace
December 2022

TABLE OF CONTENTS

Introduction 1

CHAPTER 1
CHARACTERISTICS & LEARNING HOW TO CARE FOR THEM 5

CHAPTER 2
HOW TO KEEP ONE AS A PET 47

CHAPTER 3
WHAT THEY EAT AND DRINK 55

CHAPTER 4
WHAT TO BE CAREFUL ABOUT & BE AWARE OF... 59

CHAPTER 5
BABY WESTERN CONIFERS AND THEIR CARE ... 71

CHAPTER 6
MY STORIES ABOUT SOME SPECIAL WESTERN CONIFER SEED BUGS 87

CHAPTER 7
HOW THEY PASS AWAY 125

CHAPTER 8
MORE STUDY NEEDED AND WHAT CAN BE LEARNED FROM THEM 133

CHAPTER 9
SPECIAL SECTION ON SHIELD BUGS AND SOME SIMILARITIES WITH THE WESTERN CONIFER SEED BUGS 135

ABOUT THE AUTHOR....................................... 163

INTRODUCTION

Love transcends all. No matter what you look like or what problems you might have or even what species you are, The Western Conifer Seed Bugs know, show, give and accept love. And you would never dream that they were or are capable of that or think or believe that they had or have the intellectual capability to do so. Society conditions us to think low of them and dismiss all intelligence, so we can just kill them. This needs to change and we need to recognize that bugs have much to teach us.

What started as a curiosity of a bug that was brought into the house because of the frigid outdoor temperature, turned into a whole world of learning, fascination and discovery. It opened my eyes to the fact that these bugs aren't dumb, stupid and worthless, just aimlessly wandering about, not having any feelings at all. These voiceless, innocent creatures have so many emotions, different personalities, reasoning, so much intelligence and also love human companionship!

It only takes a very small amount of time for them to realize that you aren't going to hurt them and they can trust you. Just spending under a half hour with them, they come to understand you are their protector and friend. They will observe, listen and learn from you, as they can be taught and domesticated. You become their entire world now, since they don't have to look out for themselves anymore and know that you are now caring and watching out for them.

Throughout the United States and most countries around the world, The Western Conifer Seed Bugs (also known by their Latin name- Leptoglossus occidentalis) habitually start arriving near entranceways to homes and around windows, when the bitter winds of the autumn start because they feel the warm air escaping to the outside and they are cold, looking for warm shelter.

At first, their appearance can seem alarming, intimidating or even threatening to most people because of two things. When

BUGS THAT LOVE! By Lori-Michele

you look at them quickly, you could think that they are some kind of spider, but these bugs have six, not eight legs. Another thing is the sound their wings make when flying, coupled with the fact that they let their last larger legs hang down and when their wings are open, they have a black and yellow striped pattern on their back, which gives the slight appearance of a wasp, and that can frighten many people. But these are gentle creatures, who love to crawl lightly on your hands or who can return to you after a flight and land with perfect ease, agility and accuracy.

When I first dealt with a Western Conifer Seed Bug, I was leery of it because I did not understand anything about this bug and had no reference guide, including information on the internet, to find out about them in detail. I gave this bug some water on the kitchen floor and was fascinated to watch it walk over to the small puddle and pull from underneath its body, a long thin straw-type apparatus, in order to drink. I later found out it is called a labium, but I will often call this a drinking straw, in this book.

I was initially afraid of just not knowing how safe it was to handle this creature. Could it bite me? Was it poisonous in anyway? How do you take care of it?

This lead to me consulting a local entomologist, at a college nearby and I asked a ton of questions, but there weren't too many answers. No one knows what they eat, except for what they are named after, conifer seeds, and there aren't any of those to be found in the wintertime. Also, most entomologists study ways of how to kill bugs, not feed or save them, so I was pretty much on my own.

Determined to care for my new-found pet, I started to give the Western conifer my own mixture of sugar water and I was told it was the right thing to do, as most bugs not only love it, but can survive on it. I only worried about making the mixture too thick, because if you do, it might not be able to drink it easily and I wanted to make sure it got enough nutrition to survive.

BUGS THAT LOVE! By Lori-Michele

The Western Conifer Seed Bug, has little fear of humans, especially when you are kind. Most will gently and willingly extend their front foot, followed by the rest of their feet, to climb aboard your finger.

After I had the first pet *conifer*, (as I sometimes refer to them for a short name title, throughout this book,) I decided that in the fall of that year, I would rescue and bring all the Western conifers indoors that flew or crawled to the doors and windows of my house, so they would be safe and warm for the winter. Soon, I had sixteen of them, but what I didn't realize, were all the issues that were ahead, that I never expected.

In this book, I will share my observations, experiences and advice with you, for keeping one as a pet. I will tell you all the different things that occurred and happened, as well as what to watch out for and be aware of, so your experiences with these bugs will go smoothly and be much better and enjoyable. But, for all intents and purposes....The Western Conifer Seed Bug is a wonderful, totally quiet, loving and kind pet, with very little mess and upkeep.

I've also included a chapter on Shield bugs and how they are similar to the Western Conifer Seed Bugs in many ways. Both of these are considered *true bugs* and they are not insects or arachnids. They are great fun to have as pets!

So enjoy reading and learning all I have to share because these are truly... Bugs That Love!

****

BUGS THAT LOVE! By Lori-Michele

CHAPTER 1

CHARACTERISTICS & LEARNING HOW TO CARE FOR THEM

When you find a Western Conifer Seed Bug or bring one into your home, some are overly-cautious and quickly flinch, in a reaction to the shadow of your hand. They are ready to run because they have been on the defense to keep alive in the wild outside world. If they are crawling quickly initially, it's usually because they are thirsty.

It can take some conifers a while to lower their defenses, until they evaluate that you are not there to hurt or eat them, but to care for them. Sometimes it takes just a few days for them to stop being scared and on the jump every minute and other times a little longer, but they are very intelligent and learn fast. If you spend a lot of time with them, they come around faster and some never fear you right from the beginning! Many come into the new environment very self-independent, but then learn, as time goes on, to rely on you heavily for their needs. Almost all become true homebodies!

Western conifers love to be held, talked to and adored. They are such gentle, loving and emotionally sensitive creatures. These bugs are willing participates to be domesticated because they are very observant and can learn in a short amount of time. They have fear and caution at first, but if you talk to and handle them gently and show them that there isn't anything to be frightened of, they will listen to you and gain confidence.

Originally, I had several that I never confined in containers and they were free to go wherever they wanted, but they learned and adapted that there was a boundary in the house. They would stay in the one section of the living room and never ventured, randomly and wildly, like a house fly, into the kitchen, bathroom or bedrooms. They seemed to know that this was the area I kept them in and they could play, live and be taken care of here, so they never flew or crawled beyond that region and stood in the vicinity.

BUGS THAT LOVE! By Lori-Michele

After they have been with you for a month or so, they fully understand that they are being cared for and looked after. They notice and watch as you change the liners in their containers and give them fresh ones and the same with their sugar water. They don't have fear anymore or want to take off flying or escape, but they do want 'out' of their containers to stretch their wings, get exercise, have better views and to be held. They realize and understand that you are there to protect them because you show that you care for them and that you will come to their aid if need be. For instance: if one falls backwards into their drinking water and is struggling to save its life and you get them out of the situation and dry them off, they know that you saved them and are looking out for them. Talking to the Western conifer, immediately after this somewhat traumatizing event, reassures and calms them and they accept your loving attention.

Gentle encouragement will give them the ability to venture forth and take that step to do what nature would otherwise warn them not to. An example is when I introduced them to a cloth bed roll. At first, they are leery to enter, but when I tell them it's okay and give them a gentle nudge on the backside or their back legs, they trust me enough to step forward, cautiously, to check the scene out first and then they realize it is safe to walk further into the bed roll. Once inside, they see that it's so nice and comfy. Soon they learn when it's nighttime, to just crawl into their beds on their own, either slowly and sleepily or a bit eagerly, but now do so willingly because they are so tired and know how comfortable their bed is! They now feel safe and secure and most don't come out for the entire night!

I've seen on a number of occasions, certain conifers that were extremely independent and I thought they'd never behave because they wanted to fly so much, but they'd surprise me after a long and wild flight, by returning to me and landing on my clothing, hand, arm or hair. Sometimes they'd even return to me by landing somewhere close to me, such as the arm of the chair I was sitting in. They seem to be telling me, "I like my freedom, but I'll conform and come back to you because you

BUGS THAT LOVE! By Lori-Michele

take care of me." I then of course pick them up and lovingly praise them for returning and they comprehend entirely that I am there to look after their well-being.

All the conifers are more relaxed and content and don't show any signs of agitation, when I put them back into their containers and cages, after they have had their flights and been held. It's like any other pet you might have…if you play with them and show them love, they are happy.

Western conifers have a gentle nature and complete understanding when you speak to them. They listen, watch and make judgment. They learn to become dependent on you and look to you as 'Mommy.' They are very intuitive and know I won't hurt them, as they comfortably stretch out their bodies and rest their little heads on my finger or hand, in complete relaxation, when I hold them. They love to be loved! And they recognize that you are caring for them and love you back!

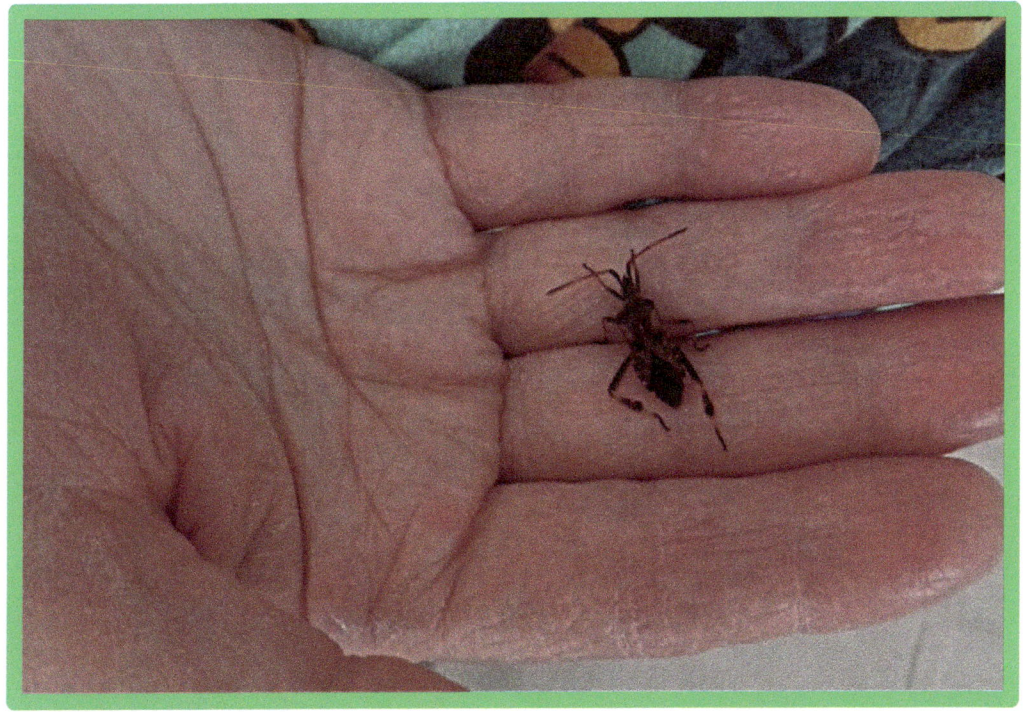

A Western conifer named Trusty, relaxing & content.

BUGS THAT LOVE! By Lori-Michele

You have to be careful to watch them at all times, because even taking your eyes off them for a moment, can lead to trouble. Since they are so lightweight and fast movers, they can crawl off your hands without you even noticing or feeling it. For instance, if you look away for a brief moment and don't feel them leave your hand, they can quickly and easily crawl onto your clothing and if you happened to lean forward in a chair and they crawl onto your back and then you lean back... or they could crawl down your leg and onto the floor and you could stand up and walk forward and just crush them accidentally... or if you lifted your arm up and then placed your arm down suddenly, on the chair or couch and they were in that exact area, it could be the end for them... and... well... any number of things could happen, if you aren't watching them intently, so be careful! Remember that you are large and heavy in comparison to them and your sheer body weight and size can injure or kill them quickly, even if it is unintentional.

These bugs are very much like humans and we share many similarities. You'll see a lot of emotional and sometimes physical comparisons, that I'll point out to you in this book.

People need to realize that these creatures share a lot of what makes us tick. We have many similar emotions, such as: scared, cautious, afraid, happy, content, bored, lonely, grumpy, frustrated, thirsty, tired, sleepy, energetic, tolerant, puzzled, loving, caring, sympathetic, etc.

They respond emotionally, just as we do. If someone is nice to you, you are more trusting. If someone is mean to you, you want to run away. They have animosity towards certain other bugs they don't like or get along with, as we don't like certain people because of their personalities. And they can have emotional problems if picked on by another bug, just as you would, if picked on and bullied by another human being.

They enjoy a tasty drink and a soft, comfortable bed, as we do. These bugs love praise, affection, encouragement, and to be happy. They love to play, groom and relax. They have good and

BUGS THAT LOVE! By Lori-Michele

bad days and they like to explore new things to stave off boredom. They feel and react to cold, heat and physical pain. And they reach out and acknowledge the comfort you give to them, near their time of death, just as a person would.

If you ignore them for too long, they will become lonely. These bugs need to be held daily and if you leave them in their containers for a day or two, it shows. Some will not drink and others will just sleep for an extended time or sit still and put their antennae down and hardly move at all! They lose their cute personalities and zest for life, as they want to be out crawling or flying or simply just hanging out with you.

I found it surprising when I took a couple of them out, after they had been in their containers a day or two, as I was simply too busy to care for them, that they just wanted to be with me. This was especially true for *Sweety*- a conifer, who would just sprawl out on my hand and sit there quietly. Then her Shield bugs pals, *Pillow* and *Easter*, would look over to her and do the same.

I thought they'd take off right away and want to fly, after being cooped up for so long. But they like to just sit with you, as you talk to them and I think they find it comforting. Some also like to stare and watch TV while you hold them and that always makes me laugh. What are they thinking of those moving pictures on the screen? But Western conifers are inquisitive and they want to check things out.

Also, some conifers kept in their containers too long, will do the opposite and speed up their walking pace, racing with pent up energy, just wanting to burst out of their cages! Many times, they have literally pushed up and against their screen tops and wiggled their way out and then flew to wherever I was in the room and landed on my hair or clothing. I swear they were trying to get my attention and wanted to be near me, so I would talk to them and let them play.

Western conifers have their own ways about them and all are individuals, with likes and dislikes. They all have

BUGS THAT LOVE! By Lori-Michele

different personalities and behaviors. Some look forward to fresh sugar water in the morning and go to it immediately for breakfast. Others like to sleep in, preferring to stay in their bed rolls and it takes a few hours for them to 'wake up' and get going for the day. They preferred to have breakfast at 11 am or noon instead.

Each one has their own particular 'thing,' such as: one will clean it's antennae a lot; crawl a lot; fly all the time; drink a lot; sleep a lot; favors a pine cone or pine clippings to sit on; wants to go exploring, etc., but universally and especially after a flight or two, they all love to be held!

Some have a spunky nature and love to spontaneously take off and fly or speed-crawl everywhere, never taking much time to slow down at all! Others like to sit on your finger or hand restfully and just be. Some like to be rocked in a rocking chair, while you hold them in your hand and others don't like the rocking motion at all and wonder with irritation, "What the heck is happening here?" And yet they can also have changing moods. On one particular day, a conifer will not want to crawl at all and the next day it'll be very active. It's as if it took the day off just to relax!

You wouldn't think a bug could get bored, but these intelligent ones do. I put pine clippings, sticks and little pine cones (a favorite of theirs) and even a shoelace, in their cage to crawl on and explore, but it only appeases them for a short while. Some will just get bored quickly, sit there and mope. They like to explore and do different things. After all, they use to have complete freedom to fly and land wherever they wanted when they were outside in the summertime, but now they are sheltered inside for fall and winter.

Usually, when you let them play for a while, they have a much happier disposition and they get along better with the other conifers in their containers. Just like humans, they need to exercise, to have a better frame of mind.

BUGS THAT LOVE! By Lori-Michele

Some of the male bugs are very gentle and loving. They like to be held and just walk around and take life in stride. Other males are pretty wild with non-stop energy and don't slow down at all!

Western conifers in general though, have less stress if another conifer or other bug is in the container with them, so they do like companionship. But if two males are in one container and they don't like each other, this can bring on more stress. An example: *Drapey* was strung out by the overzealous and wild *Dryer* who ran around on the top of the screen all day and everywhere in the container. Drapey, who was a calmer bug, started to extend his male appendage, as a warning to Dryer to stay away from him, but this put Drapey under a lot of stress. When I removed the 'wild' Dryer, after a while, Drapey would return to his normal self and his appendage would go back in and he would be calm again. So, just like people, some can drive you nuts with their behavior and stress you out!

Also, if you are too aggressive with them, they will fear you and cower or simply stop walking in their tracks. They can become bullheaded and if they don't want to be gently pushed to walk straight ahead, such as, if you wanted to assist them in getting to the water dish, they will simply freeze in place, lower their bodies to the ground or kick their back leg out against your finger as a way to say, "Go away, I'm not taking a step further!" or "Leave me alone, I'm staying right here!" They can become very stubborn. They have a mind of their own and they use it!

These bugs are instantly judgmental when they see for the first time, another bug of their kind, just as we humans make an assumption of one another, the first time we see someone else. I have had females like or hate each other immediately and the same with males. When they get along, it's like watching a good friendship. They don't bother each other, they give each other space, they are friendly towards each other, they eat together and sleep next to each other. I was surprised to see a female conifer *Ribbon*, who was alone and wanted attention, cuddle up next to another female conifer *Flippety* after they were put in the same container together for just a half hour. They became instant friends.

When Western conifers don't like each other, they attack each other quickly, usually one more dominate and stronger than the other, but sometimes they can be equal in size and strength. And when they make their minds up that they don't like each other, they rarely ever change. Sometimes though, after a week or two of hating each other, they call a truce and get along and some even become good pals!

Another thing is that because of the situation of being placed together in a single container or cage, some of the conifers bond and become buddies. It's something that I believe just wouldn't happen out in the wild. Some of them really take to each other right away or after a while, learn to like each other. Then they depend on each other for friendship and company. It's comforting for them to know and see another conifer is there with them and they aren't alone. I feel that by having two conifers in one container, it puts both of them at ease and helps them adapt to their new way of life.

A word about bullies and a change of attitude.
When several female bullies are placed into a cage together, the toughest ones, will put the weaker ones into submission. An example: a female conifer that picked on a couple of other females, will now be picked on by a tougher female conifer and she will then cower.

This can also go too far, where a tough female will be picked on by one or more tougher females and then have a sudden personality change and be so submissive that she will hide a lot and not even go near the drinking cap.

When this happened, I removed the suddenly defenseless one and put her into a group of friendlier females. Sometimes they learn their lesson and become nicer and don't return to bad behavior. Other times, they will regain their bad behavior of being a bully and start to pick on the friendlier females. Another 'go round' in the bully cage can sometimes straighten them out and they learn that being a bully isn't right. Other times, they just stay a bully for life.

Yet, sometimes bullies can change, as a person can, for the better. *Big Girl* was definitely one of the bullies, but after she was held and got more attention, her behavior, attitude and personality changed. She didn't seem as smart as the others, but she certainly had more compassion than any of them, which I learned later, as she faithfully stood by and next to her roommate *Magic*, who was dying. Then Big Girl went through terrible depression for two weeks and had to learn to adjust without any other conifer for companionship, as she was the last one to survive out of the entire group of conifers from the year previous. She had lived over a year and outlasted everyone else- both male and female.

Big Girl now came to rely and depend on me a lot and got extra sensitive to everything. She needed reassurance and to be held more, just so she'd know everything was alright.

In her 'older age' she lost her balance more and would fall off my fingers and into my palm or fall off my clothing. She'd also fall over a lot, when walking in her container, but was still quite active. She would stay on her cloth bed till noon every day and then walk around in her container and up the sides of it, until 6 or 7 pm, stopping once and a while to groom all her legs and antennae. And I'd take her out of her container a few times a day as well. She liked being held every night and then would just sit on the top of her bed at 8 or 9 pm, until I put her into her bed roll at 10 pm.

In another case of bullying, *Wee Willie*, a small, black-colored baby Shield bug, had crawled up the legs of the Western conifer named *Cookie*, then onto her back and up her antenna and then onto her back again, but wouldn't get off! He clung tightly and changed position, as Cookie desperately tried to push him off her. He repeatedly did this every time he was walking by and saw her. With this bad behavior, I removed him from the container.

BUGS THAT LOVE! By Lori-Michele

One day, I put him into *Cookie* and *Wendy's* container, just so he could get a drink. When he finished, he started heading in Cookie's direction. She saw him coming and she turned all the way around to put her back to him because she never forgot what he did to her several times and that he was a troublemaker and pest. Cookie was mad and disturbed. When I removed Wee Willie from the container, Cookie became more relaxed and returned to her normal temperament and became her old self again! She even went and got a drink.

It shows us that bugs certainly don't forget who or what bullies them. They become upset when they see their enemy, just like humans, and Cookie tried to avoid the confrontation.

Cookie, Wee Willie & Wendy

Dominating behavior. Western conifers for the most part do not habitat together and so when you put them together in a cage or container, with all females or all males, sometimes a strange thing happens. They still have sexual urges and they will try to mate with each other. This occurs mainly with the bully

BUGS THAT LOVE! By Lori-Michele

bugs, whether they are male or female. They jump on the other one for a while, but they have the wrong sex, so nothing is going to happen and then they move on. I also feel it can be a dominating thing as well, to tell the other bug that they are stronger than them and they are the ruler in this cage. Some bullies do this once and a while, while others never stop doing this and just seem to have a mean streak, picking on the others.

Yet, sometimes you'll see a conifer resting half on the back of another- both males or both females and they'll just be sitting there, relaxing and hanging out. I think this is sometimes just a way of being together, with no dominance or sex involved at all.

They can be jealous of other conifers and act out to get your attention.
Tagger had the container all to himself initially, but then because I had so many conifers that kept coming to the door that winter, I ran out of room. I had no choice but to put two other male conifers in with him and he didn't like it one bit. He tolerated his new roommates, but when I let them all out to play, Tagger could be free again to be himself and he didn't like sharing me with them.

One day, I was holding both him and another male bug in one hand. Tagger saw me stroking the back leg of the other male bug (the only way you can really pet these bugs) and he wanted the same attention. So he approached the other bug and walked around him and then lay right next to him because he saw my finger and felt that if he was next to that other bug, he'd get the same treatment and he did! He liked having his back leg stroked as well and found a way!

Ginny, a young, new female conifer was especially jealous that I lovingly talked to the older and slower conifer, *Big Girl*, who had lived a year in the house. So to get my attention, she would walk over to Big Girl and crawl on top of her, because she knew I'd get annoyed and push her off. She'd do the same thing, if I held both of them in one hand. But, if I wasn't around, she'd just walk all around the container and not bother Big Girl at all.

BUGS THAT LOVE! By Lori-Michele

Ginny wanted all the attention and didn't like that I gave Big Girl more. And she recognized that I was punishing her for bad behavior (by pushing her off the other bug), but that didn't mean she was going to change!

They know & love play time.
All conifers look forward to you holding them and then flying around a bit to get rid of their nervous energy.

Riffy loved to take off from my hand and do a backflip onto my upper body. She would do this over and over, as I collected her from wherever she landed on me. And she could do this endlessly! She loved to play and have fun!

When I put three female Western conifers and two Shield bugs-named Pillow and Easter, on my bedspread, Pillow got so excited he started to propel and flutter his wings at a rapid rate, like he was going to fly, but he was just exercising his wings because he was so happy to be out and play! Most of the time, both the Western conifers and Shield bugs walk and follow the whole length of the striped pattern of my bedspread, not aimlessly crossing over or walking any which way. It's amazing to see and it suggests some other kind of intelligence to be able to follow and stay on course of a striped line!

BUGS THAT LOVE! By Lori-Michele

Shield bugs- Pillow & Easter following the striped line.

Friendly loved running the length on the top of the sofa chair and when he got to the end and disappeared out of view, I saw his antennae moving all around as he was thinking of where he was and what he should do next. He couldn't see me at all, so I called out to him over and over and when he heard me, he slowly turned around completely and crawled back up to the top. As soon as he saw me, he started running towards me, across the top of the sofa chair, as I cheered him on. When he got close, I placed my hand out, so he could crawl onto my fingers quickly and I praised him.

We tried it again and this time when he got to the far end and disappeared from view, he just automatically turned around and came back toward me, as I was cheering him all the way!! He loved it because it was such great fun!! And we played this little game over and over again. He enjoyed being independent to walk where he wanted and he knew I was watching out for him and then when he heard me calling him, he'd turned around and came race-walking back to me!

Western conifers are adaptable to routine, such as a specific time to awaken, eat, play, and sleep and that amazes me. If you choose to get them up in the morning at a specific time and open the drapes to have the light shine in, they might not get up 'rarin to go,' but they'll eventually start to crawl around.

If you choose to feed them at 7 am or 8 am, etc. they will adapt and actually look forward to seeing you give them their sugar-water dish for breakfast.

They learn what time you will take them out of their containers to play. If you choose late morning, afternoon, late afternoon or early evening, they remember that time daily and start crawling around a lot because they're getting excited, that they'll be let out soon to play.

If you choose to have them sleep at 7, 8 or 9 pm and put them in a room, while they are in their containers and turn out the lights at that time, they will go to sleep.

And some even adapt to a routine if you want to hold them and spend time with them, watching TV at night, before you put them to bed. They will stay still in the palm of your hand and/or watch TV with you!

They have the same needs and behaviors when it comes to the weather, as we do, even though we are about 100,000 times bigger than a Western conifer! When it's hot out, we are uncomfortable and tire and can get physically sick from the heat and so can they! A lot of the time they will slow down and rest, but some get so sick, that the heat can almost kill them! I've had to pour cool water on them, when I was without an air conditioner and the place got to be over 90 degrees. They tend to stay on the bottom of their cages to stay cool or if there is a fan on, they'll stay on the screens at the top of their containers. They even enjoy being held in front of a fan, at a distance, but this can also 'dry' them out too much with just fan air, so you have to be careful not to put them in front of it for too long.

In the wintertime, they like to stay warm and cozy like we do, but remember that they don't have clothes on, so they can be even colder than we are! When I pick them up, during that time of year, they like to flatten and stretch out in my warm hand, like it's a heated bed. I have also put them on a piece of cloth and then onto my warm computer, where they all stretched out and enjoyed the warm and thorough heat. And just like we love to put a warm blanket around ourselves on a cold night, they love to hide and keep warm in a bed roll made out of a polyester fleece-type cloth.

These bugs have a memory. Once, a male conifer- *New Boy*, somehow climbed up and out of his plastic container, even though the sides are slippery and they can't grab with their feet too well on this type of surface. He walked onto the table and over to a small pine cone I had placed there, that was a distance away from his container. It was the very pine cone that I had given him to crawl and play on in his container for several days. He recognized it and climbed up onto it and stood there. He equated that this was a safe place to be and he didn't crawl any further. I don't know how long he had been out of his container, but I discovered him sitting there on the pine cone, when I walked back into the room. He wanted to be found and he didn't dare to crawl further and get lost. He knew the pine cone was a safe place to be and that he'd be found by me eventually. How cute is that?!!

Maybe, who I had since she hatched, remembered that I put her into a cloth bed with the rest of her sisters and brothers, as she was growing up and everyone stood inside through the entire night. As an adult, I put her into the cloth bed at night and she always stood there until the morning.

BUGS THAT LOVE! By Lori-Michele

I noticed one day that she remembered where her water dish was and exhibited frustration that it had been removed. I had taken it out of her see-through screening cage and placed it on the outside temporarily and then I removed it from there as well. But, she remembered where I had placed it and later she walked over to that area. Then she kept crawling up and down the side of the screened cage where she last saw the water dish, looking and looking for it.

When conifers learn where their drinking water is, they don't forget. Whenever they are thirsty, they just automatically know where to go to get a drink, especially after you teach them where their water dish is.

All of them knew that the yellow dish I provided had sugar water in it. When I took it away for almost a day and then put it back in, one started race-walking straight down the side of the screened cage, as I was putting the water dish in and went right up to it and got a drink.

One night, I showed Zippy how to go into a bed roll, which he was unsure and scared of, but I gently nudged him in, as I talked to him, to tell him it was okay. He stood in the roll for a while, but was soon back out and he climbed up onto the screening of his container. Since it was late, I went to bed and assumed he'd just stay on the screen. But when I got up in the morning, he was missing. It had been a cold night and Zippy remembered that I had put him in that cozy bed roll and didn't forget. I looked closer and there he was, inside the bed roll, keeping warm!

Bad behavior is learned with peer influence, just like humans. *Ballerina* was a tough old girl and when I put *Riffy* in the same container with her, since another female had died, she took to developing a dominant behavior and jumping onto Riffy, to control her and say, "Hey, I'm the boss here!" Soon, Riffy, who always had a calmer, happy-go-lucky attitude, suddenly began to copy the bad behavior and started jumping onto Ballerina.

BUGS THAT LOVE! By Lori-Michele

Riffy's demeanor changed dramatically and she was now intense and dominant and she flew away every chance she got when I held her, whereas before, she always did little 'hop-flights' and lovingly returned to me all the time!

When bad behavior is learned, it can't be unlearned for quite a while. Riffy continued her new, learned, dominant bad behavior from Ballerina and then acted it out, when I put her into a container with a mild female named Mini. I had to push Riffy away from Mini every time she misbehaved until she learned it wouldn't be tolerated.

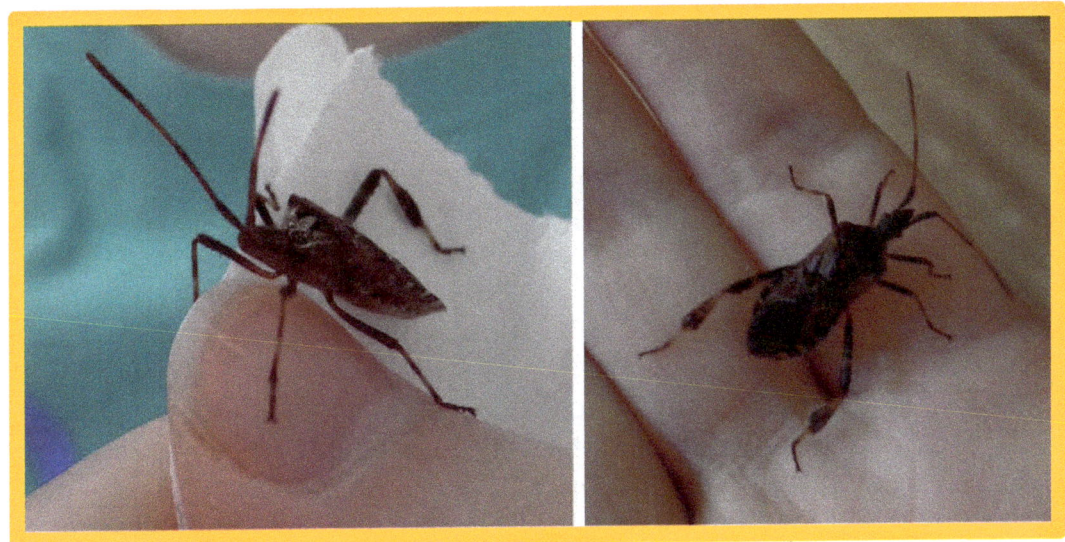

Ballerina & Riffy

Western conifers seem to have guilt and shame for their bad behavior if they fly off and get lost, when I finally come to find and get them. Body language-wise, they know they disobeyed and were scared they'd be out on their own again and away from the comforts of play, food and a nice safe container and bed. They eagerly or shamefully crawl back onto my hand, antennae lowered a bit, as I gently talk-scold them about going where they weren't suppose to and they seem to understand that they went too far. Most will just stay in my hand and nestle, happy to be back in security, found and saved. Others will not learn their lesson, behave for just a short while and then fly off

BUGS THAT LOVE! By Lori-Michele

again!

Even though I put them back into their container, as a form of discipline for not behaving or being too wild, they still willingly crawl back in, as they come to know and understand that it is also a 'safe house.' Others don't see it as punishment at all, but seem to be relieved, especially if they get lost and then found, that they are safe once again in their little home.

Their intelligence is greatly underestimated. I think it's hard for us humans to even believe that a bug so small, usually under an inch long, and with such a small head and brain, can be capable of thinking, reasoning, evaluating and then making decisions!

Here is an example of one being so smart. One time, I let a female conifer out and she flew to the ceiling lamp and around it several times and then landed. Most of them don't fly off into another room, so I ignored her for a short while because they just like being out of their containers and being on the warm glass lamp shade. Well, when I looked up later, she was gone. I got the flashlight and searched everywhere, but I couldn't find her. So I sat down and just looked over at the multitude of small containers that I kept all the conifers in, with their screen tops and there she was... sitting on top of her screen, wondering how she could get inside!! She actually knew exactly which container was hers and flew to it and waited... after she was done with being out and up on the ceiling light!

Some Western conifers have higher intellect than others and will show you that by demonstration. One male bug flew off and I tried to find him fifteen minutes later. I went over to a table and was looking down and picked up an object to see if he was on it. The bug had been watching me from a plant next to the table and deciphered I was looking for him and so he flew out a bit from the plant and back to it, to signal me. I turned and saw him and as soon as I put my hand out towards him, he flew into my palm, so happy to be back with me. Then he remained there and stretched his legs out in comfort.

BUGS THAT LOVE! By Lori-Michele

They come to know their given names. They respond and perk up when I go over to their containers and talk to them. They will even crawl over to me as I talk to them, hoping that I will take them out. When I take off the screening, some are so eager to be with me, they stand up and balance on their back legs and wave their two front feet in the air, for me to pick them up first, similar to a puppy dog! When I put my finger in front of those waving feet, they eagerly climb aboard! They crawl up your shirt and sit on the top of your shoulder. Some like to crawl and play with your hair, which is fascinating to them. Others get frustrated by it and just like to stick to crawling on fabric and material.

One time, while I was holding *Maybe*, she communicated with me, to tell me she was thirsty, by extending her drinking straw straight out and down, over my first finger and left it that way. This is rare that a conifer would do something like this and I was surprised. I brought her over to the sugar water and she started drinking. How did she know by doing this gesture, I would understand what she was trying to tell me? Remarkable, isn't it?!!

Peppercorn had flown to the Christmas tree and climbed up high onto the lighted star. When I held my hand up to him and waved, and told him to fly to me, he looked down at my hand and seemed to understand the command and took a leap of faith, jumping off the tree and trying to fly to me. He didn't quite make it and landed in the pine needles and branches of the tree about a foot down from where he'd been. Determined to try again, he turned around and climbed quickly back up to the lighted star. Again and again, with perseverance, he tried to jump off the star and fly to my hand, but he'd miss and land on the branches below. Even though he failed in these many flying attempts, he once again climbed up the star with unwavering determination, but I took pity on him for all his attempts and got closer, so he'd just be able to crawl onto my finger.

The fact was, that he understood my command and was trying to get to me and couldn't, yet he never quit. This shows that the

BUGS THAT LOVE! By Lori-Michele

Western conifers have mental endurance.

Comprehension, trust and decision-making abilities.
I have watched the decision-making abilities of the conifers and it is so intriguing. For instance: *Ballerina*, ventured off her little bed cloth, that I had placed on my thigh (while I was sitting down) and she walked as far as to the end of my knee and sat there looking over. Then, she decided to turn around after several minutes and walked straight back and onto her bed cloth, where she knew she would be safe.

If a conifer is on your hand and reluctant to leave, such as stepping forward onto material that they are unsure of, but they see your other hand nearby, a couple of inches away, they will then have the confidence to go forward and crawl to the other hand because they recognize and trust that a 'hand' is security, safety and you!

One day, I found a new conifer on the bathroom wall in February. I just reached my open hand up the wall as far as I could and started talking loudly up towards it, coaxing the bug to come down. Remarkably, it understood me! It turned around and looked down and started walking towards my hand. It went slowly, as it didn't want to lose its grip on the wall and it seemed a bit frightened, but it overcame that fear and somehow it knew that I wanted to help it and I could be trusted! It inched itself a little at a time down the wall, heading straight towards my middle finger that was closest to her. It could have veered in any direction, away from me, at any time, but it wanted to come down to me. She then confidently crawled onto my finger when she reached it and I pulled my hand down and away from the wall, as she went along for the ride and knew she was safe.

How could a bug so small, comprehend, assess and instantly trust me and then make the decision to come down towards me, knowing I'd take care of it?!! It absolutely amazes me!!

She stood on my finger and then in my palm and cleaned her antennae confidently. When I placed her in a container and

BUGS THAT LOVE! By Lori-Michele

gently nudged her toward the water dish, she obeyed and then happily and quickly started drinking for over an hour.

After nine years of having these little creatures in my life, I still wonder how something so small can make an instant judgment about a human, that is huge in size by comparison to them and just 'know' that I'm not going to eat or harm them and then trust me! How intelligent these bugs are, yet no one realizes this at all!!

I've come to hate the saying "What a dumb bug!" because most people don't realize that they are anything but dumb. They think, comprehend, analyze, make decisions, give effort, have compassion and trust and so much more!

When you make them your pets, you will come to love them more and more and believe as in any love for a pet, that they are smart and loving and respond to you. For all intents and purposes that is true, but some people will believe that you 'see' more in your pet then there is...intelligent wise.

There will be some Western conifers, especially if you have several, whose personalities will just shine more than others. You might notice that one responds to you more or you might recognize that one is more intelligent or has more personality than the others. This I noticed with only a handful of my favorites. They were far superior in intelligence to the others and naturally I favored them, but I loved them all.

BUGS THAT LOVE! By Lori-Michele

With the intelligent ones, they become easily bored and love something new added to their containers or cages. I put an empty red cap into the cage as something colorful for *Big Girl* to just look at. She'd walk over to examine it and sometimes I'd see her crawl onto the side of it or into and out of it, since it was rather large. Then one day, I looked into her cage and wondered where she went, because I didn't spot her right away. And there she was inside the red cap, making it her little bed to rest in for a while.

You'll also notice that after you have your conifer pets for a while, they'll start to get spoiled. They adapt to the comfort and living in a domesticated world and they get spoiled streaks of behavior. They suddenly won't want to do as you say so readily, like getting a drink or even coming out of their containers to play. Whatever mood they are in, will dictate if they will be cooperative or not, as well as their general personality.

These pets know who you are and they will not stray far from you when they do their flying...well, the ones that really like you. They will fly up and around the ceiling lamp and then when you walk under the lamp or nearby, they will zoom and land swiftly and accurately on your clothing, when they are done flying. Some will rest a bit in your hand and go off on another flight, but will return to you once they have had enough and are tired.

If you are ever looking for one that seems to have suddenly

disappeared on a flight, you can rest assured wherever they are, they see you! They have extremely accurate vision!

After everyone has had their flights and exercise, I put them back into their containers and they are all tired out and content. Later on, they'll get a sugar drink. They become very adept at their new life and some get very spoiled, but they are just so cute, you forgive them for everything!!

Eventually, after you have them for months, they simply don't want to fly anymore. They don't lose the ability, they just don't have the need to fly and seek out food anymore because it is now always provided for them. Sometimes, they still do little 'hop-flights' as I call them, flying just a short distance from your hand to your clothing or about a foot from one part of you to the next. And they enjoy crawling so much, that they get plenty of exercise that way.

When they don't want to go back into their containers.
Many come to learn quickly that going back into the container means they won't be with me any longer to be held or played with, so they grip my finger tightly and make body movements to tell me they do not want to get off and go back inside, when they see me lowering them into their container.

A lot of the time they simply don't want to go back in because they feel the half hour or more that I spent with them, just wasn't long enough to be with them! They will back up on my finger and/or turn around quickly and try to climb the other way. They will grip my finger tightly, as I try to gently push them off with the other hand and they will out-step me! The feet that I do manage to push off, they will use the other feet, to get a better grip and/or crawl under my finger and do everything possible not to be nudged off. When I am finally able to manage getting them completely off my finger, some will mope and be depressed that they are back in the container because it's boring. Sometimes, though, when they see me lowering them into their containers, they'll adopt an 'I'll be good attitude' and won't move, believing if they don't crawl or fly away, then they'll be able to spend more time with me. And I must admit, they were so cute when they did this, that they won out and I spent more time with them!

Others will happily and readily walk off your finger because they want to go back, as they have had enough play and exercise and remember and recognize the comfort of their soft beds. They will then start to 'wash up' and clean their legs and antennae, walk around inside their container and maybe even get a sugar drink, as they are at home completely!

They love human companionship.
One Western conifer named *Friendly*, loved to be with me and would hang onto and stay on the middle of my shirt for many hours. I could work on my computer or walk around the house and he'd happily hang on, just to be with me. Some get really attached to you and want to be with you a lot for company. He would always climb up the side of his container constantly, until I lifted him up and out and then he'd become all content and happy.

Friendly just resting.

BUGS THAT LOVE! By Lori-Michele

Sweety also loved to be out and with me, crawling on my arms and hands as much as she could. She even liked to crawl up onto my shoulder and just sit there and look at the world around her. At night, when I held her for a while, she liked to rest in the crook of my hand, between thumb and forefinger.

Sweety, feeling completely safe, sleeping on my hand. When the Western conifers are sleeping, their antennae are in the horizontal position.

Henry was quite bright and he would listen to me when I would call to him, if he went up too high on the drape. He'd look back at me, then turn around and come crawling down to me. I would praise him for returning and then he'd love to snuggle on my fingers or in the palm of my hand, where he'd stretch out, like a dog would do in front of a warm fireplace, to relax and be completely comfortable and content. He always felt safe there and would stay quite a while.

BUGS THAT LOVE! By Lori-Michele

Henry relaxing.

In your busy schedule, it can be difficult to tend to so many conifers and give all of them attention. But even holding them for fifteen minutes a day, can ease their anxiety and comfort them. Ideally, having two to four conifers can be well-handled, but I made the choice to take on all that came to my door one season and that lead to sixteen! Trying to give all of them my attention became a bit challenging, but I made it work by letting four female conifers out at a time to crawl around on the comforter of my bed, to get their exercise. It is easier if you have a large area like your bed or large table, etc. to keep watch of them easily, while so many are out playing at one time. And remember, some do not like or get along with others and crave individual attention. They want to be your special one!

When Western conifers are completely happy, relaxed,

BUGS THAT LOVE! By Lori-Michele

content and at peace, they will often start to groom themselves while they are on your fingers or palm of your hand. And this is the number one sign that they are relaxed and comfortable with you and feel safe and secure. They tend to 'wash' their hands first, by expelling some liquid from their drinking straw and rubbing their front feet together and then they 'comb' or 'wash' their antennae next, by bringing them forward and down and patting them from the top part near their head, all the way to bottom end, one at a time. Some start at the middle point of their antenna and work the rest of the way down. Most tend to start with the right antenna first, which is similar in a way to us humans, who are mostly right-handed. Then, lastly, they clean and wash all their feet, the second and third pairs, as they rub their feet together, two at a time and sometimes three!

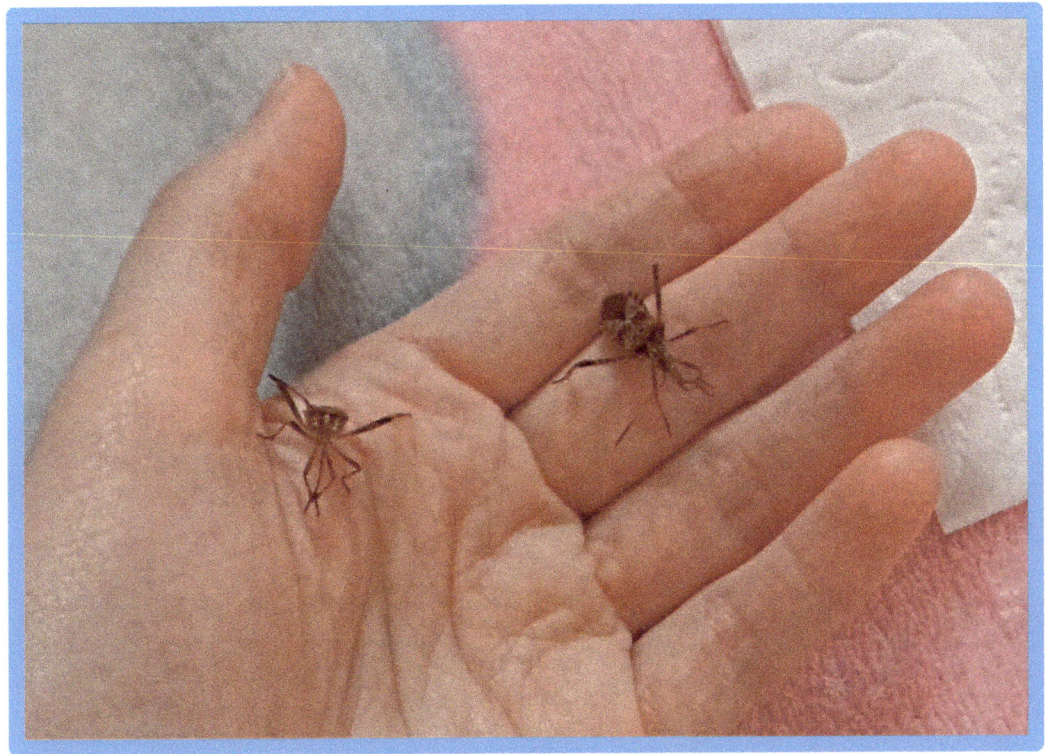

Two Western Conifer Seed Bugs washing up on my hand.

BUGS THAT LOVE! By Lori-Michele

Front view of Western conifer washing up.

They like to bask in the sun and I believe that they get their vitamins this way. Bring them to a sunny window, whether you leave them in their containers or take them out. Place them in an area where the sun can shine down into their containers or let them crawl around on the pane of a shut window, making sure it's not too hot. Many enjoy this sunning and sit still, but others will simply crawl around and not even bother to bask. If it's a particularly hot day and the sun is beaming hot, be careful not to let them sit in the sun too long. For those days, about five minutes should be good enough. Some sun is good, but too long and hot of a sunning, is bad.

They have an automatic built-in emotional behavior that is instinctual. Most won't and don't pee on or in their beds. Most will back off their beds, to pee on the paper, when they feel the urge come on. Almost all of them do this automatically from the time they are babies and it continues on into adulthood.

They also relearn and override their natural instinct and become docile. By nature, anything that touches their back legs is cause for alarm. But through repeated, gentle touching on the side of their back legs, they learn that it is my way of giving affection and they learn not to be afraid. It is easier to pet their back legs than their back, which all conifers take as threatening or uncomfortable.

A rare thing that can occur, when holding one of these conifers, is that they can 'hum.' You'll feel their bodies vibrate and it's obvious it means something. Sometimes, I like to believe that they are trying to talk to me or convey that they are happy and calm, such as when a cat purrs.

One irritating thing for a Western conifer.
They enjoy crawling all over your hands and clothing, but none of them likes walking on the hairs of your arms. They find this difficult, confusing and irritable. I suppose they liken it to some kind of uncomfortable, stiff weeds from the outdoors, who knows? But they don't like it and it slows down their crawling, as they try to navigate over it.

Nighttime survival.
Now having these conifers double-up, so-to-speak (having many live in one container together) can be aggravating, especially for males. They are dominating by nature and so they sometimes lunge forward towards one another or walk over each other or jump on one another and even try to mate!

But after attacking one another and being aggressive during the day, at nighttime, it's a different story. They will all group and huddle together, especially on top of a screen to their holding container, upside-down, touching each other with their legs. This could be because they remember nighttime brings danger, when they lived outdoors and so it is a survival technique of protection in numbers. Staying together in a group, they'd be less likely to be attacked by enemies. They might hate or bother each other in the daytime, but at nighttime, they put that all aside and get along together, to protect themselves from the 'unknown enemy.'

Sometimes the females do this as well, grouping together on the

BUGS THAT LOVE! By Lori-Michele

top of their screens or huddling together inside a cloth bed roll. I wonder if any of these conifers have a memory of when they were babies because baby conifers will huddle together to keep safe when they are out in the wild and in captivity.

Accidents can and do happen.
Even when you try your best to be careful, accidents can and still do happen with these bugs, whether it's your fault or theirs. Here is one short story.

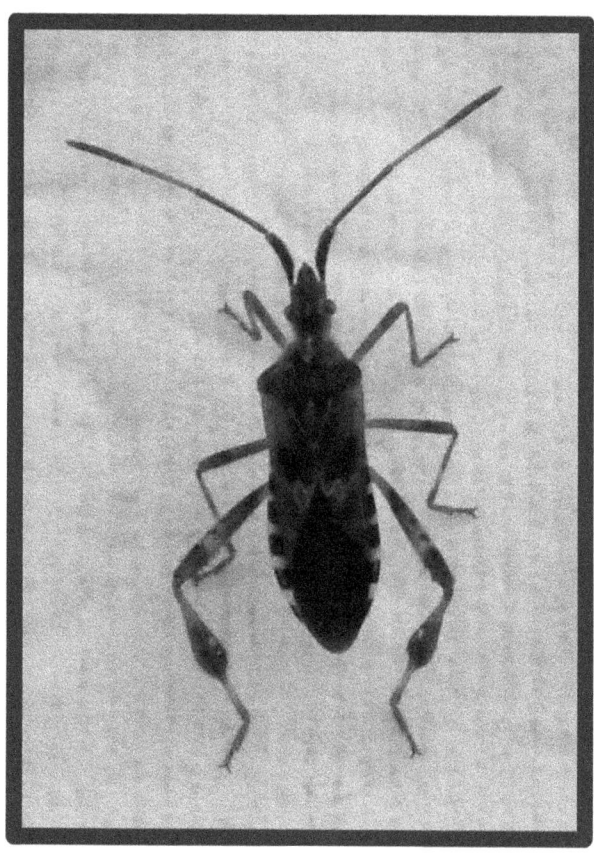

Peppercorn was very independent and you couldn't anticipate his next move. He'd be quiet and calm and want to just sit with you and in the next second he'd fly off and disappear. This became a habit and unfortunately, very frustrating because he'd hide so well. He wouldn't just reappear and fly quickly again or be like most of the others, who flew away initially and then would fly to a light source or a wall or the drapes. He'd fly to wherever he wanted and I'd find him eventually, in all kinds of odd places- under the mini-blind, the underside of the windowsill, the side of a bag, on a plant leaf, under a table or at the side of it, on the heater baseboard cover and so many other places, including the floor.

No other conifer ever landed on the floor before and so I was worried about this behavior. He, however, knew where he was and often could see me, but I couldn't see him and he knew this. So, after hours of being 'gone,' he would suddenly fly in front of me to get my attention.

Once he did a short flight from my computer, where he was perched, but I didn't see him, over to the printer, as if to say, "See, I'm right here!" Other times, I'd hear him fly by me and then I'd look in that direction. Most of the time he'd be gone for hours and sometimes a day or two! I was always happy to find him and gushed praise all over him, and he'd like that, but would want to fly again and do the same behavior all over again!

One day it led to disaster. I had him out to play and crawl up the pull strings of the mini-blind, which he liked to do. Then I heard him fly off and crash into something. I looked and looked endlessly, but couldn't find him. Still, I was pretty confident that he'd show up in an hour or two.

When a couple of hours passed, I got worried and looked more and kept calling his name. I walked in and out of the room several times and on one of those occasions, I'm assuming he attempted to fly to me, as I left the room. He landed on the rug in a very dark section of the entranceway between the two rooms and when I walked through again, I stepped on him and didn't know it.

I noticed something on the rug when I was leaving the room and bent down and gently picked it up. Peppercorn was loose and limp and when I placed him in my palm, he was upside-down and looked like a spider when it's flattened out... a bad sight to see. I quickly turned him over and assured him it was ok, as I believe he was in shock. He slowly came around, but he just sat with his antennae up and he didn't crawl or fly. He used one of his back legs to wipe his wings and it looked to me like he wanted to get them open and apart, but couldn't. His body didn't even look like I stepped on him at all and he wasn't crushed. His drinking straw was fine and in working order and all his legs worked as well.

BUGS THAT LOVE! By Lori-Michele

I held him all day, giving him encouragement and he drank some water. At night, I put him on top of his cloth bed and hoped for the best. But, the next day, Peppercorn seemed to be drinking for hours and then he gave up and his antennae went down. He did have damage that I couldn't see. I held him for nine hours, to give him comfort, as he started to pass and felt very bad that the accident had occurred in the first place.

Emotional problems can occur with the death of a pal.
Secret started off as a 'don't touch me' kind of bug. He was a big male and very independent. He got his name because I couldn't tell what sex he was and he didn't seem to have the tell-tale sign of the male bump on the underside backend of his abdomen. I kept him in a small container and then one day, a week or two later, he revealed he was a male by sticking out his appendage, when he was on the screening.

I then put him in a container with *Cautious*, a smaller male with a missing leg, who got his name from his behavior. He must have never forgotten what happened to him and how he lost that leg in the wild, so he was extremely fearful and cautious about everything.

At first, they stood away from each other, but later Cautious developed his sense of security and became more aggressive. Poor Secret, he was a bit intimidated by Cautious and when he came around, he'd get out of the way quickly or let Cautious walk all over him. It was clear who was boss in this container.

Still, Secret enjoyed crawling all day long on the top of the screening and oddly, after a couple of weeks, the two of them became friends and got along perfectly. They would drink from the same water cap and they'd sit next to each other, on the top of the bed roll during the day and go inside it to sleep at night. It was cute and amazing at the same time, as most male bugs do not get along together at all!

But then, after several months of perfect harmony, Cautious died suddenly and Secret was emotionally lost. He had bonded

BUGS THAT LOVE! By Lori-Michele

with Cautious and they were close companions. He was now all alone in his container and depressed.

I thought I could fix the problem by putting him in a container with another male bug, but it didn't work. Either he'd attack the other male or the other male would attack him. One time, I found a male conifer on top of him and Secret on his back, in an all-out fight. The other bug somehow broke Secret's upper front arm and now he was limping around holding it up high in the air. He could still move the arm, elbow to wrist, but couldn't bring the rest of his arm from the shoulder, down.

Secret was now running away in the container constantly, in fear of the other male bug and simply petrified. I had to do something, so I put him in his own smaller container. This didn't help much, as he got depressed again. He wouldn't drink from the clear-colored water cap anymore, so I had to get a blue-colored one and he finally drank. Then he developed a nasty habit, that every time I held him, he'd bring his labium forward and stab me. He wasn't thirsty, but I'd catch him moving it all around on my palm, as if he was. (Note- some do this briefly just to smell you.) Then he wouldn't drink from the blue-colored cap anymore, so I gave him a red one and then he'd just leave his drinking straw hanging down into the cap of sugar water most of the day, which was odd. I wondered if he was so bored, that he'd just do that to keep busy.

Days later, when I put him in another container with a gentle male, he ran away in terror, never forgetting that the previous male hurt him badly and broke his arm. Another time, I had that same gentle bug walk by him on the sofa chair and even though he lightly touched him with his antennae, Secret jumped and turned around in fear. Nothing could shake this fear, even with me there, telling him it was alright. I felt bad he didn't have anyone to look at and play with, but he couldn't be in any container with another male, from then on.

He liked to be held, and learned that he could only be held, if he didn't attempt to hurt me with his labium. He liked to just sit on the arm of the sofa chair to be near me and watch me, for a sense of security. Then he'd go for a bit of a short walk. He became extremely attached to me and when I tried to gently nudge him off my finger or palm, he'd hold on with all his might because he didn't want to go back into his container, all alone again. Secret became so sensitive and an entirely different bug since his partner Cautious died. I feel he developed all these behavioral problems because he lost his best pal.

Finding them outside in the dead of winter.
Sometimes you'll notice a Western Conifer Seed Bug outside, in rain or snow, clinging to the house, window screen or screen door. Usually the temperature is too cold and the brutal elements of the weather take their toll on these poor bugs before you can save them.

I brought one inside, that had been clinging to the side of the house, in the pouring rain and freezing cold, but even though it warmed up inside, it still passed away.

This also happened to another one I found outside on the window screen, in the dead of winter in January.

The weather had oddly warmed up to almost 60 degrees one day and then turned cold very fast, as the temperatures plummeted and nightfall came. Soon, brutal pouring and freezing rain, pounded outside and then snowfall started.

The next morning, I saw the conifer on the window screen at 10 am. It had its antennae bent all the way forward, and it's feet were tightly wrapped around the small holes of the screen, as it desperately had clung there in an attempt to stay warm. Some ice had formed on it, but the conifer was still alive.

After bringing it in and thawing out, it just relaxed completely on the soft piece of toilet paper, but the night had been too brutal and it slowly died.

The only peace I had with both of these bugs, is that they

passed away in the comfort of the warm house, on a dry piece of soft toilet paper, with someone who talked to them, touched them and cared about them. To die alone, outside in those brutal elements with no one around, is just too awful for me to think about.

Luckily, not all the stories about finding a conifer outside in wintertime turn out badly.

I just happened to look out the window one mid-February day and saw a conifer lying right on top of the snow, with its antennae straight forward and down. It looked frozen and wasn't moving.

My father went outside and scooped it up and then I took it and started to dry off the snow, as it melted into water on her back. Ice crystals were all over her legs, but one by one, they melted and turned into water and I dried each one off. She responded quickly and started to move her legs and came back to life. I guess we saved her in the nick of time!

She had bad coloring when she was brought in, extremely light brown, like she had already passed, but a day later she was walking everywhere and her darker brown coloring returned. What a difference a day makes! We named her *Snow*.

A word about disabled, lame or maimed bugs.
Disabled bugs, both Western conifers and Shield bugs, learn to adapt and know you're there to care for them. Never discount a disabled bug, thinking that: they can't care for themselves; that their life will be unbearably hard and that it simply isn't worth caring for them; or that it would be best if they just died.

I've had several maimed bugs and while I would have rather had them mostly perfect like all the rest, so many of these bugs taught me so much. First, that they are survivors. Second, that they adapt to and overcome their disability. Third, that they are smarter than the others because they have to adjust to their impairment and find ways to do so. Fourth, that they are just as

BUGS THAT LOVE! By Lori-Michele

loving and sometimes more loving, than the other conifers. Fifth, that they can live just as long or longer than the average conifer. Some have come to me with missing legs or a half of an antenna, yet they go on and live just as the others do. *Zoomer* lost a front leg and yet she adapted and used her first left foot and her second right foot to clean her antennae. And although they can be a bit clumsy walking, when they lose a leg, they still march forward and go on. There is no self-pity. They deal with what is missing and adapt.

Others have had accidents in the house, for which I have been responsible and then felt terrible about it. This was the case in which one conifer was on my pant leg, but I didn't know it and when I swung my legs over from one side of my bed to the other, I inadvertently took off two legs and injured two other legs so badly, he could only move them minimally. He was left with only two legs that worked. This is why I stress it's so important to be aware of where they are, at all times. They are so small in size, that sometimes it's hard to see them.

Troupey, the bug I accidentally injured, would be extremely depressed when left in his container and his antennae would droop downward, but he'd be very happy with his antennae held high when I took him out. He would grip his front leg over a piece of bent toilet paper, that I'd prop him up on and he loved looking out and over at everything that was happening all around him in the room. He stood all day on the arm chair where I placed him and it was very important to him to watch everyone and the goings-on of the day and still be very much a part of life.

Different species that accept each other. We all get along, but you just don't know it!
You'd think that all bugs are independent and for the most part, while surviving outside, they are. But when they are indoors and in the comforts of your care, they still can and do become lonely.

What I found surprising, is not only do they love companionship of another bug of their kind, but if you can't provide that, (for

BUGS THAT LOVE! By Lori-Michele

reasons that you don't want to pair up a couple of the opposite sex and you can't tell them apart or that you run out of containers because you are taking so many bugs in at once) they welcome another species of bug wholeheartedly!

The assumption we have about bugs in general, is that they don't get along with another species of bug. I also, believed this to be true, until I had run out of containers to keep both the Western conifers and Shield bugs separate.

Although I was leery at first, I had to place a Shield bug, *Bugaboo*, in with two male conifers and to my surprise, they got along! They'd feel each other with their antennae, to check each other out, but neither species saw the other as a threat or attacked each other. It was quite fascinating to see.

After a week or so, all three were on the underside of the screening, placed on top of their container and they were next to each other, placing a foot or antenna on the other bug. This is a sign of complete acceptance of each other. It's amazing to watch and see how they all get along while they are in the same container together. They are surprisingly adaptable and they have intuitiveness in distinguishing foe or friend.

Bugaboo & two male Western conifers.

BUGS THAT LOVE! By Lori-Michele

Because both of these species are always out in the open and flying, it would be hard-pressed to believe that they'd ever come in contact with each other in any other way, but being placed in the same container, they had no choice in the matter. They didn't become fast friends, but they gave each other space, and they respected each other. They didn't pick on or bother one other and all of them lived in harmony. The Shield bug would get a drink from the water cap, at the same time a Western conifer would. And they all shared the same bed roll, especially when it got cold out.

I never expected two different species of bugs to accept one another, but they co-exist quite peacefully and accept each other for who they are. People don't realize that these two species of bugs have gentle, loving and kind natures.

Then I tried putting three different bugs in one container together: a Western Conifer Seed Bug, a Boxelder bug and a Shield bug. They too, respected each other and got along so well, they started acting as if they were siblings. One would step on the other to get a drink and the one who was being stepped on didn't mind or flinch because he knew the other was just doing something innocent and not harmful in anyway.

A Western conifer & Boxelder bug (top) and Shield bug.

BUGS THAT LOVE! By Lori-Michele

I watched the Boxelder bug and Western conifer touch antennae and stay next to each other on the screening and then walk around together all day as buddies and that was something to see!

The most species I've had in one container was four: a Western conifer, Shield bug, Ladybug and Boxelder bug. I watched the Ladybug crawl under the back legs of the conifer to feel safe and then later, I saw the conifer walk up to and rest next to the Ladybug, even though there was plenty of room in the container to rest anywhere else. These four distinct bugs all drank together at the same water dish, at the same time and remarkably, they even shared the one bed roll together!

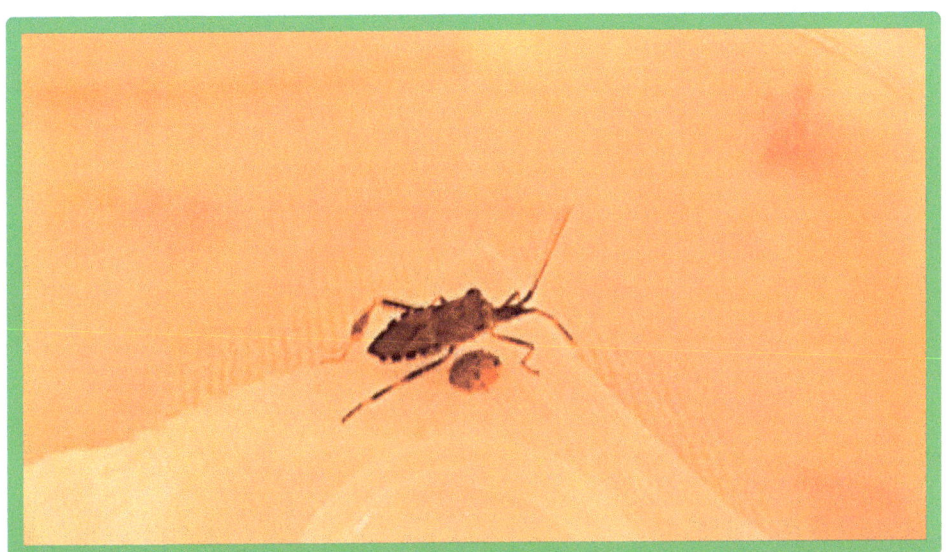

A Ladybug feeling safe under a Western Conifer Seed Bug.

I've observed all these bugs intently and I've studied their behavior towards one another. It is quite extraordinary that all these different species of bugs are so loving and that they want and willingly accept companionship. They truly enjoy each other's company!

Also, if any one of the species of bugs, has any number of missing legs, a missing foot, half an antenna or is disabled in anyway, all the other bugs wholeheartedly accept it. They do not

BUGS THAT LOVE! By Lori-Michele

discriminate against any other bug that might have it a little harder than them, as everyone is considered and treated equal.

Harriet, Applejacks and Polly-Molly. Note that Harriet has a disfigured wing, but it didn't hinder her flying and the other bugs accepted her warmly.

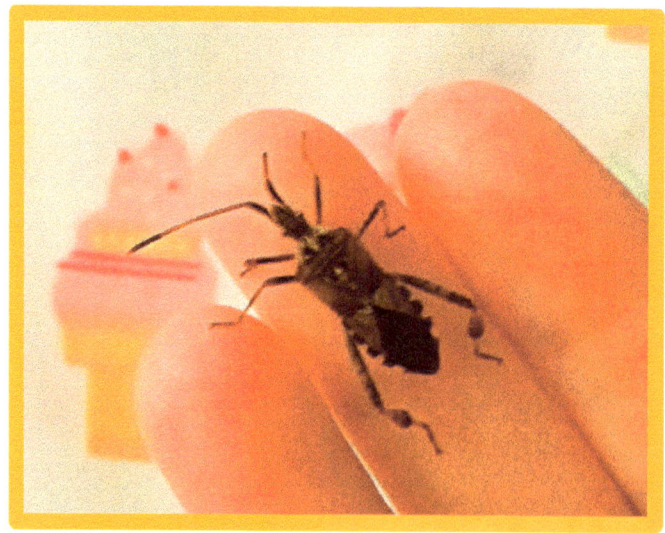

Here is a photo of Peace, who arrived with only part of an antenna. He was a very happy bug!

BUGS THAT LOVE! By Lori-Michele

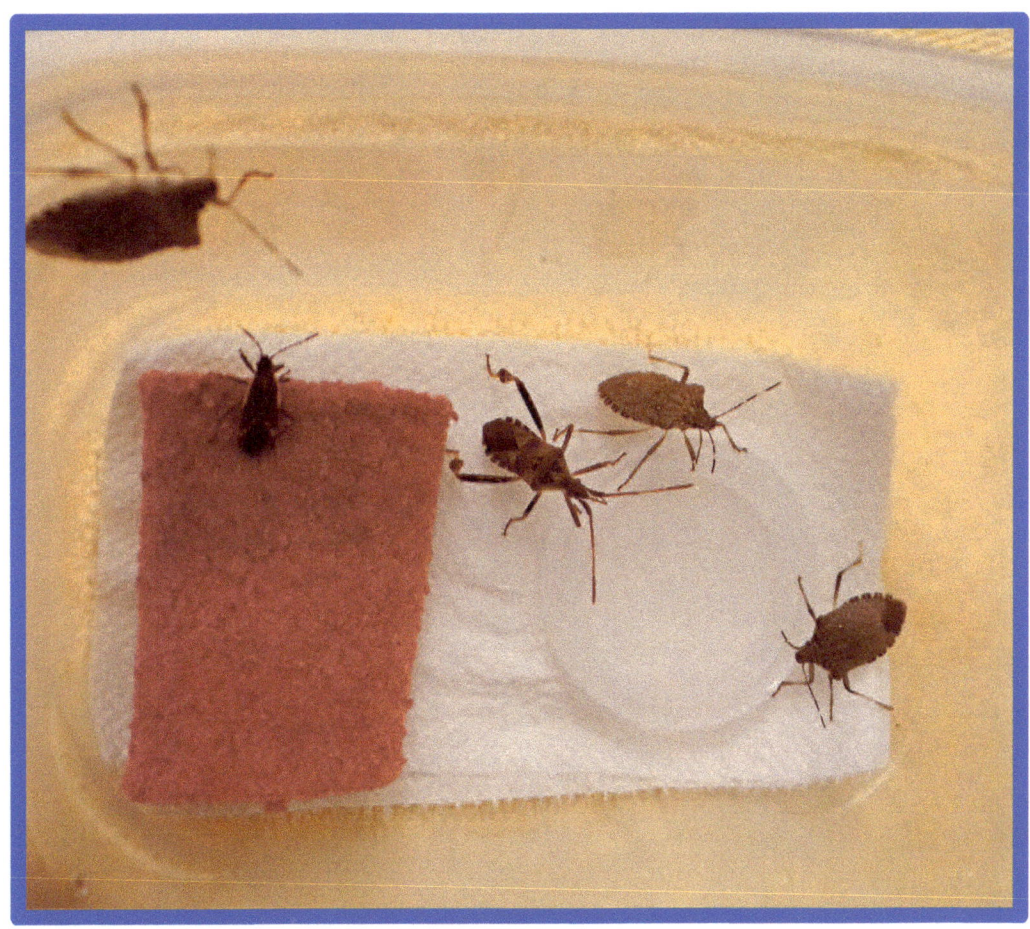

Everyone getting along together, in one container, to play and drink. Three different species; a Western Conifer Seed Bug, 3 Shield bugs & a Boxelder bug.

*A quick note- Houseplants can be poison to some bugs, who stab into them and try to drink the liquid in the stems.

Sassy, the Boxelder bug, got lost for a few days and then I finally found him. But he was weak and ill, as he had stabbed and drank some liquid from a houseplant. He kept wiping his drinking straw with both front feet over and over, so I assumed he had some sticky residue leftover and couldn't remove it. His behavior was off and I knew he was sick. I had to hold the little sugar water-filled cap for him, while I encouraged him to drink,

BUGS THAT LOVE! By Lori-Michele

which he did for an hour. It took a day or two for him to become normal again, as he had to clear the poison from his system, but it did shorten his life and he passed just a couple weeks later. So, be sure to keep your Boxelder pets away from houseplants.

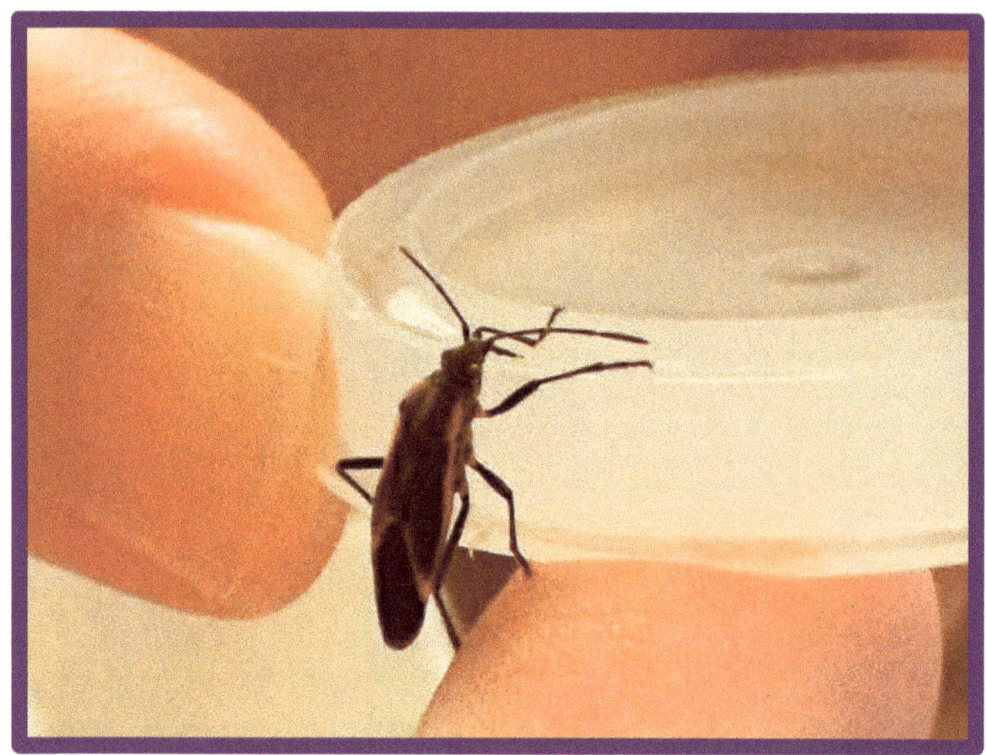

Sassy being hand-fed to clear the poison from his system.

BUGS THAT LOVE! By Lori-Michele

CHAPTER 2

<u>**HOW TO KEEP ONE AS A PET**</u>

It's pretty simple to keep one of these harmless, little creatures as a pet. For the Western Conifer Seed Bug, you can use see-through plastic food containers to keep them in, such as: a one cup size or an even larger, but flatter one. For the top, a simple piece of soft nylon screening, that you can get at your local hardware or big-box store, will do. Just cut the piece of screening to be a little larger than the width and length of the container, so it will balance and stay flat on top. This will allow you to easily open and place it back on the container, each time you want access to your conifers. You can use paper, toilet paper or Kleenex® to line the bottom, but the last two are quicker and easier to replace often.

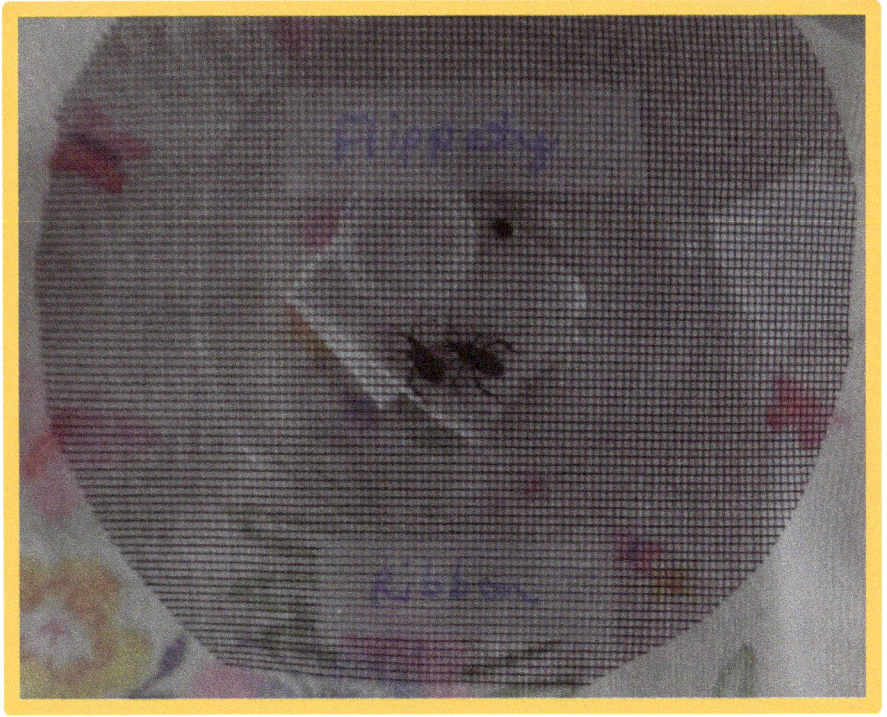

A top view of a one cup size plastic food container, with oversized nylon screening on top. You can also put labels on the top with the names of your Western conifers.

BUGS THAT LOVE! By Lori-Michele

Make sure to keep your containers in an area where the easy-access screen tops will not be knocked off by bumping into them or by a strong wind from an open window or if you close a door too quickly.

Another type of cage, which allows them more freedom to crawl and get more air, is to create a rounded or semi-square type structure out of a piece of nylon screening. Make sure that you cut a piece that is a perfect rectangle- 8 inches high is good and about 26 inches long and when you have the two ends meet, line it up and tape across to secure it. Also, tape the inside of the screen where you joined it together from the outside, so when the Western conifers crawl up the inside of the screening, they won't get their feet stuck on the sticky tape from the outside, that is now facing in towards them. Place it upright and check to see that there are no gaps underneath the screening, on the bottom because the conifers will innocently crawl out through the bottom if there is a gap space.

The harder part is affixing a top to the screening. I placed a piece of 8 ½ by 11 inch, 20 lb. printer paper on top of the screening that I bent inwards. I flipped the whole thing upside-down and placed it on a table. Then, I taped the screening to the paper from the inside.

For this larger-type cage, it's best to place a piece of paper on an end table and put the cage on top of it. This way, you can change the paper easily and frequently. And for extra fun, you can use colored papers for the holidays, such as: light red for Valentine's Day; light green for St. Patrick's Day; light pink for Easter; light yellow for spring; light orange for Halloween & Thanksgiving and green for Christmas or light blue for Hanukkah.

BUGS THAT LOVE! By Lori-Michele

A larger homemade cage with nylon screening and a paper top (left) and a one cup size food container (right) for quick & easy housing.

They will need some kind of water dish and a plastic bottle cap lid will do- preferably a flatter one, for them to drink from easily. I use the ones that come from a one gallon plastic water container. Make sure that there are no sharp edges. The higher the cap, the more difficult it is for them to lift their drinking straw over the rim and into the cap to drink. But, sometimes you can accommodate this, by using a folded up piece of toilet paper or a cloth next to the higher cap, for a 'boost' so they can climb onto that and then drink. (Try to give them a "fresh" cap every day in the summer, so the sugar water doesn't become tainted with naturally occurring bacteria. Sometimes, just dumping the water out daily is still not enough, to clear bad bacteria off the cap itself, so a new one is best.)

BUGS THAT LOVE! By Lori-Michele

Some have a difficult time seeing the clear plastic caps and will try to stab the side of it, instead of lifting their drinking straw up, over and into the cap. Colored caps sometimes help them to see and understand where the water is a little better. And you can teach them where to get a drink, by putting a little sugar water on the tip of your finger and then touch the tip of one of their antennae lightly, while they are next to the cap with sugar water in it and then put your finger over or even into the water to show and teach them, "Here is the water." They seem to understand this gesture and learn from it and then remember where they can get a drink.

I like to give them a bit of the outdoors, to feel at home and they enjoy a thin stick or two to explore and walk on and some pieces of greenery, such as snippets of an evergreen bush. Little pinecones are a favorite of theirs, to inspect and crawl on. And you can even put a soft piece of yarn attached to their ceiling and let it hang down for them, to play with. They can become bored, so these little objects help them adapt to their new environment, especially since it reminds them of where they use to live.

A Western Conifer (center) crawling up yarn in cage.

BUGS THAT LOVE! By Lori-Michele

Also, being a girl, I like to spoil them and I have never forgotten my childhood days of when I dressed up my dolls and then later, my pet animals. So, I didn't think it was fair for the Western conifers not to have a soft and comfy place to sleep and I decided to give them little homemade beds. A simple piece of cloth, cut rectangle-size, that you can make a circular roll out of it. No need to tape or sew it, just make the ends of the cloth overlap a bit, where they meet together and you can place it down into their holding container. They like to crawl into this bed roll, whenever they want to rest or to keep warm, whether it's daytime or nighttime. I trained them to go into it at night, just before I turned the lights out, but many crawl into it on their own will.

Amazingly, they seem to sleep as long as I do and then they are up and about, when I get up in the morning. But sometimes, if they don't want to get up early, they won't! When it's especially cold, they slow up their activity considerably and some will stay in their beds all day and night. They prefer a warm and cozy cloth, such as a fleece-type polyester during the wintertime, but something cool and light, such as a rolled piece of toilet paper or a light sheet material, for the summertime.

A Shield Bug sharing a summertime bed roll with a Western Conifer Seed Bug.

BUGS THAT LOVE! By Lori-Michele

Also, if you keep more than one as a pet and they are the same size and sex, it might be difficult to tell them apart. I used a safe way of marking them and you might try it as well. Get a little bit of Diaper Rash Paste (I used the generic house brand with 40% Zinc Oxide) and put some either on your finger or the end of a Q-tip® and then gently pat it onto their back foot or leg. They'll flinch at first, but this will not bother or hurt them. They might try to rub it off with another leg, but it won't come off. It'll dry to a light white mark and you'll be able to know who is who! I never put this on their backs, as that would hinder their ability to fly.

You will find yourself favoring certain ones, according to your personality or theirs! You will observe which ones are more aggressive and which ones are gentle and kind. Then, you might put them into categories. For me, there were: the bullies- ones that step all over the others with total disregard for another or intentionally jump on the others' backs to dominate and control them; the kind ones- that just mind and go about their own business just being themselves; and the special ones- extraordinary Western conifers that actually try to communicate with you and respond when you talk to them and that you have a great connection with. These ones can express themselves better than the others and 'tell' you what they want or what they are thinking, through physical gestures.

Initially, I said to myself that I would just house all the Western conifers I took in, over the winter months and release them back into the wild in the spring. But when spring came around, I felt differently. How could I let them out into the elements of the wild again, when they came to enjoy and depend on me for all their needs? When we bonded and they saw me as 'Mommy' now? And how could I let them out to be instant bird food with all the wild Blue Jays attacking everything they saw, to feed their hungry babies? I just couldn't!! So that's another thing to think about when you bring them in for the winter. You might think you're just being kind and saving little creatures from the cruel, bitter, cold winter, but you soon come to learn about their personalities and they become your pets with all their cute ways,

BUGS THAT LOVE! By Lori-Michele

as you love them more and more!

Since the Western Conifer Seed Bugs are so kind and gentle and just love to crawl, you can easily use your hands to keep track of them. You can reposition them on your arms, legs, clothing or anywhere you'd like them to crawl and they will crawl in that direction. So playing with these creatures is easy and you don't have to be extremely mobile. Of course, this becomes possible after they no longer want to fly, which is pretty soon after you care for them. You must be gentle and not rough when handling them because they are delicate creatures.

They make excellent and wonderful pets for everyone, including: any child who is kind and wants to hold and love one and take care of something small; anyone who can't speak or hear, as these bugs make no sound and you don't need to speak to them or hear to communicate; the elderly, disabled or chronically ill, as not much energy is needed to care for them; most who are confined to a bed or who have limited mobility; anyone who can't chase after or lift a regular pet, such as a dog or cat; anyone with allergies to most pets; and anyone who wants a pet that doesn't make noise or a mess or who can't have pets because of regulations where they live.

These bugs understand how much you love and care for them and they enjoy being with you! If you can hold one in your hand, then you can have a Western Conifer Seed Bug as a pet!

BUGS THAT LOVE! By Lori-Michele

CHAPTER 3

WHAT THEY EAT AND DRINK

Eating and drinking are basically the same. They use their labium to stab conifer seeds, pine nuts and other wild outdoor vegetation, to drink the liquid inside, through the stylets that are inside the labium. Drinking water is very much the same as if you or I were using a straw.

I have had many of these as pets and each generation that I bring into the house every fall season, seems to be different.

One year, I had Western conifers that just loved the pine nuts that I bought at the grocery store and they couldn't get enough of them! They would stab and try to drink the oily liquid in them for hours on end and most of the time, all day, until they became totally exhausted. Unfortunately, they became too addicted to them and I had to take the pine nuts away, just so they'd drink some water!

Some conifers seemed to pass away just weeks after eating the pine nuts and I wondered if they had chemicals on them that caused this to happen. I learned that if the pine nuts come from foreign countries, they use pesticides on both the trees and nuts, so try to buy organic ones. Also, the conifers' labium's take a beating trying to stab the nuts, even when I semi-crushed the nuts first. I noticed one conifer had a cracked labium after eating pine nuts and I didn't know if that was the cause or just a coincidence, at the time it happened.

The next generation wouldn't touch the pine nuts and preferred only sugar water and lived quite a long time on just that alone.

Western conifers don't like if you leave their sugar water for three days in a row and don't change it. Some will not even go near it because they know when the sugar water has 'gone bad' and is rancid. Some do still drink it because they get desperate and have no choice. But they all know and recognize, when they watch me give them fresh sugar water, that it's now time to

BUGS THAT LOVE! By Lori-Michele

drink up! Soon they all come over quickly to have a nice, fresh drink and enjoy it thoroughly!

One time, I tried to give some Western conifers diluted honey and they not only didn't like it, but felt like a dirty trick had been pulled on them! They had seen it as complete betrayal, as if I had poisoned their only food source, and by the very person they trusted! They had the look of "Why would you do such a thing?!" It took a while to get them to trust the water dish (with just regular sugar water in it) and me again.

When experimenting with trying to offer them different liquids, it's best to put a drop or two on the top of their screening, on their holding container. This way, if they like it, they will take a sip from there. Some like the juice from canned apricots, peaches, or pears. And sometimes they get so spoiled by these sweet drinks, that they don't want to go back to drinking their sugar water from the cap!

They do benefit from fruit juices, health-wise. I gave one conifer that was a couple days away from dying, some cranberry juice with just natural sugar in the ingredients. (Don't give them any juice with artificial sweeteners in it.) He liked the taste of it and he seemed to perk up for a short while.

Another time, one of the conifers seemed to be omitting a 'death' odor, that some have a few days to a week before they pass and especially after, which smells like a combination of pistachio nuts and old, dry and decaying leaves. But I gave him canned apricot juice and then canned peach juice frequently and not only did the odor go away, but he lived on for almost four more months! I think the nutrients in those juices healed whatever might have been wrong with him.

I did try to give the Western conifers pieces of raw zucchini one time, but they weren't interested. I put a slice of fresh apple in their containers, as well as slices of peaches, but only a select few would have a quick taste and then walk away. One enjoyed a grape from a can of fruit cocktail. It can't hurt to try different

BUGS THAT LOVE! By Lori-Michele

soft fruits, to see if they like them.

I'm still curious to know what else they eat for nutrition out in the wild, so I could duplicate it, but no one seems to know the answer. It has been said that they also like the nectar from inside wildflowers, but it is difficult to know the ones that are safe enough to try and which ones they would like best.

Sugar water is still the simplest and easiest way to go. Trying to mix the sugar water just right, can be a bit difficult, but with a little practice, you can manage it.

I was told to mix it like you would for a hummingbird, 2/3rds water and 1/3 sugar, but it's really a judgment call on your part. I wanted them to get enough sugar for nutrition, but I had to make sure I didn't add too much sugar or the water could become too thick for them to drink up the thin stylets inside their labium. If you make it too thick, they will try to drink it anyway and then give up or you might be fooled into thinking they are drinking (because they keep their labium in the water, whether the sugar water is perfect or too thick), so you have to find the right balance. They can become easily discouraged and then won't attempt to drink anymore, if they keep going to their water dish over and over, trying to drink and it's just too thick for them. And remember… always use bottled water!

I changed their sugar water often, never less than two days in winter and every day in summer because it evaporates in the hot heat. Standing sugar water thickens on its own, no matter what the temperature, but it is especially important to change the sugar water daily in the summer and even give them a new 'fresh' cap. I use the flat caps on one gallon plastic water bottles because the caps on other water bottles are too high for them.

Sometimes the bad bacteria, naturally occurring from the sugar itself, can attach itself to the cap in only two days, so if you just add in new sugar water, it can become rancid to them, from the bad bacteria that remains on the cap. Just dumping the old sugar water out of the cap daily might not be enough. A new cap

BUGS THAT LOVE! By Lori-Michele

and fresh sugar water daily, is your best bet.

If you can't get a 'new' fresh cap, you can wash the cap you have, with soap and warm water, but it must be thoroughly rinsed, to remove all soap residue and thoroughly dried, to remove any chlorinated water that remains, before you add fresh bottled water and sugar.

BUGS THAT LOVE! By Lori-Michele

CHAPTER 4

WHAT TO BE CAREFUL ABOUT & BE AWARE OF

I assumed that all the Western Conifer Seed Bugs, that I brought into the house during the fall months, were females. I had put them all together, in a homemade cage of nylon screening and a paper top. When I saw a couple of them mating, it was a shock. They literally 'hook up' end to end and stay that way for 12 hours. So, I had to find out how to 'sex' them.

Both males and females look very much the same. Don't believe what they tell you about males being smaller. They do come in all sizes and I have had small females and large males and vice versa. The only way to tell if the bug is a male, is to look for a bit of a rounded bump near the underside of their backend, by looking at the side of them, while they stand or walk. The female abdomen is usually all smooth and you won't see the little bump that indicates a male.

Another way to tell the difference between the sexes, is that at some point, most of the males will 'show it.' They glide this drawer-type shelf out, to reveal their penis which is inside this drawer. I've had to isolate ones that I wasn't sure about, until they did this act. It isn't too often, but it's hard to figure out why. Are they feeling sexual? Sometimes, if two males are together, they do this as an act of aggression to tell the other, "I'm the bigger, tougher, stronger one…stay away!" And they also use their back legs to rub this area once and a while.

BUGS THAT LOVE! By Lori-Michele

Identifying a male conifer. Note the drawer-type appendage on their backend.

After mating, it's about two weeks and the females will lay their eggs. I had made little open cloth bed rolls (open on both sides), for them to crawl into at night, to feel safe and warm and they took to this very quickly, eagerly and well. When it came time to lay their eggs, the females did this on the inside of the cloth roll, in a straight line chain. They typically do this on the underside of leaves on the trees outside, but they made do with the cloth bed.

I was surprised to see the eggs- very small, half-barrel shaped and so many of them! They will lay any number of eggs, a tannish color, depending on their genetics and size of their bodies. They can lay just a couple, which is usually rare, but all the way up to 30! The chain I counted was 16!

I was unsure if they'd hatch. After all, it was now in the deepest of wintertime, but in the warm heated house, I guess it didn't

BUGS THAT LOVE! By Lori-Michele

matter to the eggs.

After I found this batch of eggs, another female laid more eggs a couple weeks later. And even though I had separated the males and females much earlier, I found out that even after they mate, some females can hold the sperm inside their bodies for months and later decide to lay eggs! (Story continues in Chapter 5- Baby Western Conifers and Their Care.)

Now caring for Western Conifer Seed Bugs, comes with a bit of a warning from me… these creatures are small!! I call them 'micro-pets,' since their body size is usually about or just under an inch long. And to own a micro-pet, takes a lot of being careful. They can suddenly lose their grip and fall. You have to be sure you are not moving too fast when walking and holding them, because if they fall quickly, you could step on them. If they are crawling all over you when sitting down, you have to be aware of exactly where they are or you could inadvertently crush them. If they went onto your back, for instance and you didn't realize they were there and then leaned back onto the chair or sofa… that could lead to disaster.

Make sure that it's not too hot in your house in the wintertime or summertime and if it is, make sure they have enough sugar water in their drinking caps and replenish it daily. Heat can cause the water to evaporate quickly. It is best to give fresh drinking water daily, but if you are busy, every two days is okay. Like us though, no one likes old, dirty water and sugar water can go bad like anything else.

Also, cold winds are not good for them, such as being near an open window, if the temperature drops into the 50s. This can be too much on their systems and will age them quicker and they could die sooner. You'll know it was too cold when they don't get out of their beds and stay in longer, instead of being up early and walking around in their containers. The cold freezes up their bodies and makes it difficult for them to move, just like us humans. Whatever temperature you're comfortable at, they probably are too. Remember though… they don't wear clothes,

BUGS THAT LOVE! By Lori-Michele

so they'll get colder.

If they escape and crawl or fly somewhere in your house, trying to find them can be difficult because of their color and how they can not only blend in with so many things in your house, but their size makes it difficult to find them because they can crawl into so many small areas. Get a good flashlight- it makes it easier to spot them. Check the floor first and be careful where you step. Don't walk quickly. If you have light-colored furniture, walls, carpet or flooring, it's easier to see them, than on dark colors. Also, it is very helpful to wear light-colored clothing, so you can easily spot them, especially if they fly on you or crawl out of your sight, but are still on you and you don't know it. They tend to blend in with dark colors, like blue, brown, black, etc.

Use simple Scotch® tape to seal any holes, gaps or spaces in the walls or around windows, baseboards or floorboards, where you think they could crawl into and not be able to get back out. It's better to be safe, than sorry and sealing up anything that they can crawl into, is best.

Also, make sure that any lamp you have, has a safe, cool-to-the-touch lightbulb. They don't often fly into open-top lampshades, but again, it's better to be safe than sorry, as you wouldn't want them to get burned or worse, if they touched or landed on a hot lightbulb.

Rarely, but sometimes, when they are new to you and if they are hungry, they might assume you're a tree and they can just 'tap' you, since they haven't been near humans before. They will innocently use the labium (drinking straw) to stab into your hand or finger, if you are looking the other way. It is <u>extremely important that you do not overreact</u> to this painful and unintentional mishap. It will feel like a needle prick, but it is not harmful or poisonous in anyway. You have to gently and quickly push the bottom tip of their drinking straw, that is now in your hand or finger and keep gently tapping it until they pull it out and away. You can even gently, but firmly, press a back foot to make them jump and pull it out quickly. But you cannot hit or smack the drinking straw or do anything to it rashly just because you're in pain because it will lead to the conifer's death. They simply don't know you feel pain and they usually do this only when they are hungry and new to you. Most know not to even try this, but on occasion, it can happen. And when you tap their drinking straw, in the unfortunate case of this happening to you, they usually remember never to try that again!

Now the reason I warned you about being careful not to overreact and damage their labium (drinking straw) is that if it gets damaged in any way, they will die. It is a pretty amazing piece of machinery, but very sensitive. When it gets broken, it can't be fixed. It is a thin, rounded tube, that is bendable in sections and 'open' a bit at the top, closest to their head. It also has a slight opening going down the entire length on the top-front of it. This is so they have leverage and flexibility to drink. It is similar to a hollow, yet firm cylinder tube, that they use to stab the conifer seeds, fruits or other things and then the four black string-like stylets inside, which fit into grooves inside the hollow tube, work together, to draw up the liquid for their food. I was told that two of the stylets are used for drinking and the other two are for spitting the liquid out, when they wash their feet and antennae. All four stylets work together, sort of like a combination of a pulley and vacuum system.

Also, if they are dropped onto a hard surface, such as a counter or floor, it can crack their vulnerable drinking straw and this will lead to their death as well. Sometimes, it cracks for no apparent reason, but you'll know there is trouble right away because they will start endlessly 'cleaning' it. Then, you'll see the black stylets, that look like fine hairs, waving about in the air. Some have control of the stylets and you'll see that they are able to wiggle the end of them. Usually, when the drinking straw cracks, they will pull the stylets out, with their own control, thinking they can fix the problem themselves, but when they try to smooth the stylets back into the straw, they can't.

The main problem is, everything is so minute, that us humans don't have tools readily available to assist in getting the stylets back into the hollow tube and there is no guarantee that if you were able to do so, the stylets would stay in place according to how and where the drinking straw cracked in the first place; if the opening was now too open for them to stay in place, so they'd continue to pop out anyway; or if the bug would simply pull them out again themselves.

As the days pass, the four stylets get worse and start to unravel and come apart. It'll appear as one thin black strand, like a human hair, but then they will separate more and you'll be able to see this, especially when they try to drink and/or you assist in putting both the drinking straw and stylets into their drinking water. Sometimes you can only visually see two or three, but there are four.

I have had this happen to a few of the bugs. The longest one to ever live with this issue, was almost three weeks. They die because they can't get the water up and into their system anymore, with the stylets now freely flying about and not properly secure inside the hollow tubing of the labium. It is very sad and painful to watch.

The Western conifers have even desperately, extended and held out their drinking straw to me, as they were begging for my help. They were all extremely patient, and bared the pain and sensitivity, while I tried to get the stylets back in because they knew how hard I was trying to repair them and they so desperately wanted to be fixed. I used the smallest things I could find to assist me- one being a toothpick that I whittled down to a tiny thinness, but everything I used, was still too big to push the stylets back into the tube.

I even borrowed a microscope to see the tube clearly and placed one conifer on her back, in an attempt to fix the problem. She patiently tolerated all the terrible discomfort because she knew what I was trying to do to help her. But as much as I tried, I just didn't have any tools small or thin enough to be successful in putting the stylets back into place and it emotionally tore me up because I couldn't repair her.

BUGS THAT LOVE! By Lori-Michele

I always wondered, aside from injury, such as dropping them on a hard surface, what would cause their drinking straw to crack. Is it lack of humidity? Does the sugar water cause a dryness? Is it old age? Is it a biological disease of some kind? I still can't figure it out and it is puzzling and frustrating.

On a different subject, sometimes a psychological issue can come up with conifers, after they've been with you for several months. All of a sudden, some can have a difficult time drinking from their water bottle cap. Instead of just putting their drinking straw up, over and into the cap, like they always have done with no problem before, they now turn their body sideways and stab the side of the plastic cap, not getting any water at all!

This was very disheartening for me to watch or understand, so I assisted them with a toothpick, gently lifting the drinking straw into the water, so they could drink. I've wondered why they do this after months of not having a problem at all and if it's a lack of nutrition that throws off their sensibility.

Please be aware that sometimes accidents can and do happen and it's best not to have the sugar water anywhere near them at night. Sugar water is sticky and deadly, when they accidentally fall backwards into their drinking cap, because it will pull and hold them down, and they won't be able to get out. Most of the time, this can happen if they lose their grip on the screening of their container and the water cap is below them. Or, if they accidentally fall backwards while climbing up the side of their container, near their water cap.

It's a pretty frightening-looking scene, to find a Western conifer on their back in the sugar water cap because all their legs are spread out and flattened, they are a darker color and have an appearance of a spider. Panic races through you because you can't believe this has happened and your lovely little pet is in a terrible, helpless state, yet you have to remain calm and act fast, to try and save their life. I was able to save some of them- it depends on how long they have been 'drowned,' so to speak, when you find them in this condition.

BUGS THAT LOVE! By Lori-Michele

So first... get them out of the cap as quickly and gently as you can, since they will be loose and more delicate. Usually, I'd just leave them in the cap, as I poured the sugar water out quickly and held my hand underneath, in case they fell out, so I could catch them.

Then dry them off the best you can with toilet paper, as it works the best to wick the water away from them. Next, blow on them to make sure they have enough air and then take the bottom of their feet of their large back legs and put them against your finger. Now 'pump' them slowly and consistently, meaning move them up and down, where the knee joints bend and go close to their body up high and then release the legs to stretch down. Keep doing this and talk to the bug, so it'll know you are there and trying to help it. With any luck, they will slowly respond by moving a front foot or a bit of their antenna or even one of the other legs. But keep working the back legs and 'pumping' them, until you see signs of them coming around. Sometimes it can take up to a half hour or even a little longer, for signs of recovery, depending on how long they were under the sugar water. Don't give up too soon!

When they do recover, everyone is relieved, but a bug that has had a 'near drowning' will not live as long as it was going to, in the first place. It stresses the bug's system so much, that even if it looks like they are perfectly fine and back to their 'same self' again, they don't seem to live as long as the others.

To prevent these 'near drownings,' I find it easier and safer to remove their water dish at night and give them fresh sugar water each morning and many actually look forward to it. It will certainly give you piece of mind, not having to worry about something bad like this happening.

Western conifers do the cutest things and will make you laugh. They like adventure and crawling on strings, twigs and things from the outdoors. But they also like to crawl on the woven fabrics of your sofa or chair, drapes and clothing. Be aware that conifers have tiny 'hooks' on the underside of their feet, that you

BUGS THAT LOVE! By Lori-Michele

can barely see, to help grip as they walk. Some materials they find harder to walk on than others and their feet will 'catch' on a material and they'll have a difficult time un-hooking their feet, to continue walking. You have to make sure they don't get too panicked because if they struggle long enough or assume that the 'material' is somehow threatening to them because they can't get their feet free, they will yank and yank and might tear off a limb or two!! It's easy enough to just nudge the bottom of their stuck foot, to unhook it, for them to continue crawling, but it's best to have them crawl on smooth fabrics that don't have fibers that stick up or catch on the hooks under their feet.

However, it's the opposite when they get older. Usually, if they are over a year old, those hooks on their feet wear out and they slip and fall more easily. A rougher fabric actually benefits them as they get older, so they can hang on better, while they crawl.

Also, when you are transferring a Western conifer of any age, from your finger to almost anything else, the nature of these bugs is to hold on with their last two legs (their feet), even though the other four are securely on something else. They are reluctant, until completely sure, to release and let go with those last back legs, as they hold on with their toes. This does not bode well in the wild and a lot of the time when you get a pet conifer, it will have one of those back legs missing. They are simply too slow to let go, with the back feet and so you have to have patience, even giving them a little nudge, to get off safely and completely.

A couple of extra things to know....When you give them different things to play with in their containers to stave off boredom, make sure they aren't sharp objects or things that they can fall off of and get hurt. Also, I have observed that conifers that are the most active and crawling constantly, usually wear themselves out and die faster than the rest, that conserve their energy. They seem to shorten their lives by being extremely active.

Since Western Conifer Seed Bugs are delicate, it's best to keep

BUGS THAT LOVE! By Lori-Michele

them safely away from any other pet you have, especially cats, dogs or birds because they might harm them, whether intentionally or unintentionally.

Also, if you find a Western conifer that is injured and scared, place it in a container by itself with both a soft toilet paper liner and a cap full of sugar water and leave it alone for a few hours. This will allow it to calm down for a while. Sometimes you have to let it be for a day, for it to get readjusted to its new and safe surroundings. Then with gentle talking and holding, the conifer will soon realize that you are there to help it. Love and care, will heal both physical and emotional injuries.

Lastly, and I can't stress this enough, please be aware of spiders!!! Spiders anywhere in the house are their enemy and it doesn't matter what size the spiders are. I took for granted that a large and flimsy spider, who had set up a web behind the TV stand, was innocent and harmless. Well, a baby conifer that I had raised to an adult and who had a gentle and loving personality, wound up having a horrible death. He was just learning to fly and wasn't so good at the landing part. He'd head towards a wall and crash into it and fall down onto the carpeted floor.

I had to go on an errand and thought everyone was safe in their screened cage, but apparently there was a gap at the bottom I didn't see and both *Button*, as I named him and another conifer, *Maybe*, escaped from underneath and went on their flying routine.

When I got back, I couldn't find him anywhere. Then I moved the TV stand and found him wrapped up tightly in the spider's web. Seems he flew to the same spot he always did and fell to the carpet and then walked a short distance under the TV stand and the spider pounced on him.

I tried quickly and desperately, to get the webbing off him, as he was still kicking his back leg intermittently. The webbing was the most difficult and thickest I had ever seen or dealt with in my life

BUGS THAT LOVE! By Lori-Michele

and I simply couldn't cut through it. I worked consistently and even put water on the webbing, but it didn't help much at all.

Poor Button, so scared when he was jumped and attacked by the spider, had put his antennae back in fear and was injected by the venom of the spider, who then wrapped his webbing all around him in that position. I tried to get it all off, but wound up breaking the tips of Button's antennae off and felt extremely bad. I was just trying to get him free, so he could be well again. He was more comfortable and secure that I was there for him when I got the webbing off, but the damage was done. The poison was eating him from inside and there was no way to save him. He died slowly and I was heartbroken.

I will never look at a spider the same way again! He attacked and wrapped poor Button viciously, more than any average spider would. So, please….look for and get rid of every spider you see in the house, so they won't attack and kill your pet conifers. Never assume, as I did, that they are flimsy and harmless…they aren't!

BUGS THAT LOVE! By Lori-Michele

CHAPTER 5

BABY WESTERN CONIFERS AND THEIR CARE

I never thought the conifer eggs would hatch, but they did and just so you know, they all hatch on the same day! It's an incredible thing to watch and you have to be around at the right time, or you'll miss it all!

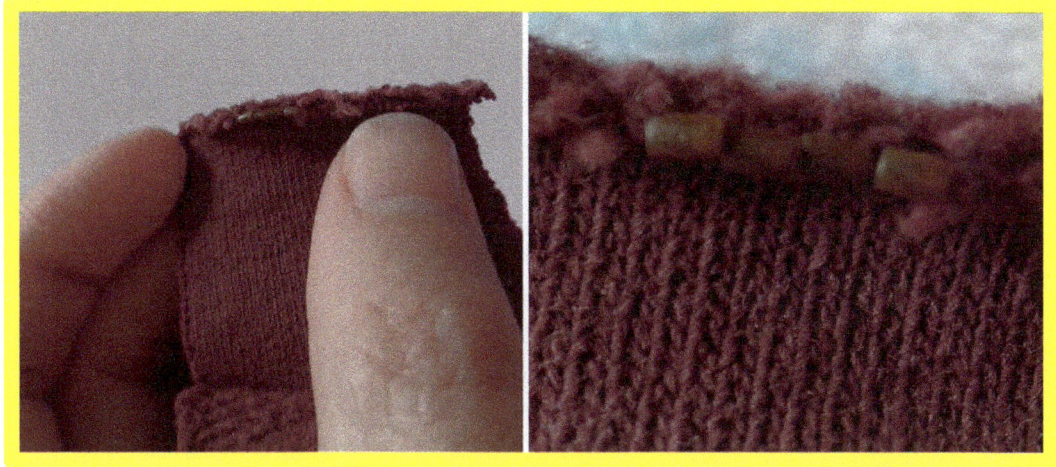

Eggs laid in a chain on inside edge of bed roll (left) & close-up view of four eggs ready to hatch.

When it's time, one will start to pop through the little egg where there is already a circular area on the egg itself for this purpose. It's like a little built-in door lid. The baby conifer will wiggle out, a little at a time, like a worm. It will get its head out first, with its little tiny eyes and then it's first two legs and then the next two legs. The antennae are folded straight down in front of their bodies, until they are almost out of the egg. Then, they slowly raise each antenna out and away from their bodies and straight up in the air and then kick the egg casing off with their last two back legs. They stand up right away and they have the attitude, as if to say, "Here I am world!" They are happy and eager to take their first steps, but are so naïve.

BUGS THAT LOVE! By Lori-Michele

Less than one hour after hatching. Notice the little door lids popped open (left) on their now empty egg casings.

They are all bright orange-reddish colored, similar to a cooked lobster shell and have black eyes, but as the hours pass, that color disappears and the body becomes darker and brownish. They have a gawky appearance, with long antennae on a small body, but they are so cute!!

BUGS THAT LOVE! By Lori-Michele

Notice how small the just born baby Western Conifer Seed Bugs are, in comparison to my finger tip.

Soon, they will start to crawl all over the place and trying to keep them safe can be difficult, especially if you don't watch them. Keeping them in a container with screening on top is still the best because they are so small and tiny, they can crawl underneath and out of other cages easily. They do become a little more active, when they are around any adult conifer because they assume it's their mother. However, adult conifers have different reactions to them. They'll either ignore them or be tolerating or give them a good, swift kick off, if they crawl onto their back legs.

After the baby conifers come out of their egg capsules, they like to have a drink, since it's pretty exhausting work! This is the first part of how difficult it is to care for these tiny baby bugs. Plain water by nature, is heavy and weighted and these babies are so lightweight and flimsy, that just stepping into the water, can pull them in and drown them quickly.

BUGS THAT LOVE! By Lori-Michele

I found a way to feed them, but I'm not so sure it was the best. I dampened a kitchen sponge with sugar water and they drank from that, but dish sponges are treated with chemicals and these babies die quickly and suddenly, without much warning. I thought that if I boiled the chemicals out of a sponge and then I let it cool and air dry, it would be safer for them, but the outcome was the same.

A word of warning about feeding them from a sponge. Sugar is both a life giver and life taker. I have found that some little baby bugs will just decide to stay on the sugar sponge in one spot, after they get a drink and then the substance hardens on their feet and when they try to walk away, they just tear their legs off! This is very shocking and scary to see….little legs left behind on the sponge. So, don't let them stay on there for a very long time!

A better way is to slightly soak a cotton swab in the sugar water and let them feed on that. And yet another way, is to soak some toilet paper or Kleenex® with sugar water and they can just walk onto that flat, damp/wet surface and drink from it. When, they get older and bigger, they'll be able to drink out of a water cap.

The baby conifers, for the most part, all stay and play together during the day. At night, I'd round them up and they'd huddle together on the soft toilet paper and go to sleep. They like to touch each other with their back legs, to tell each other, "Hey, give me some room here," in a nice, polite way, so that they can all position themselves comfortably next to each other.

BUGS THAT LOVE! By Lori-Michele

New to the world on the first day, they all start to groom their antennae.

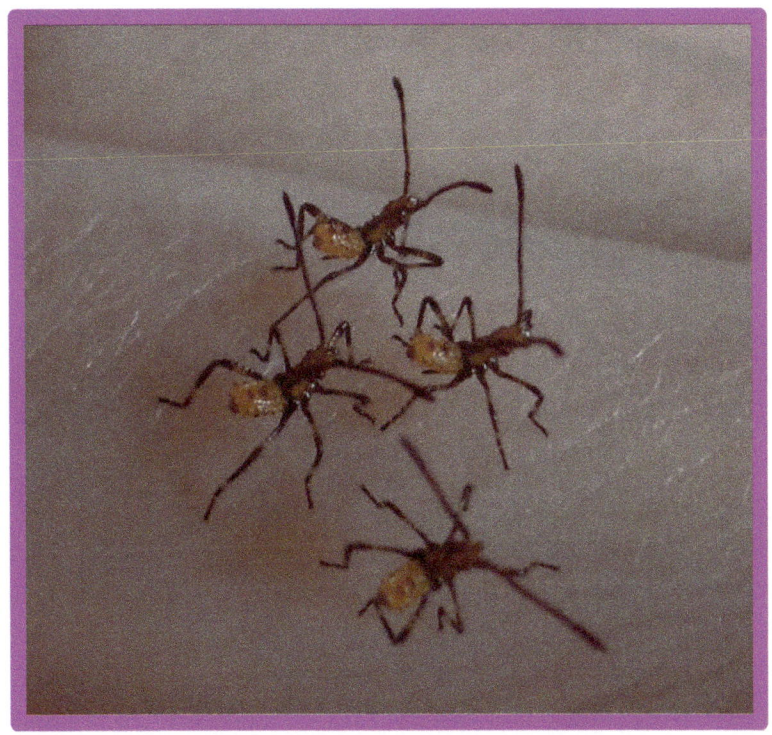

Just hanging out together.

BUGS THAT LOVE! By Lori-Michele

One day, without warning, I noticed that one wasn't walking all over happily, but had slowed down considerably. Then it wasn't drinking and its antennae start to droop down at an angle of 180 degrees.

Many baby conifers will lose strength and die in a day or two, for unexplained reasons. I witnessed with all of them, the same thing that happens with the adults. It's as if a key in their brains had been turned off, telling them not to drink anymore. Their antennae get thinner on the tips and the length and for most, their abdomen starts to shrink and get smaller. (Although some have not had their abdomens shrink, but they succumbed just the same.) Then, they start to turn black in color. Eventually, they stop walking and collapse, as their legs fold under them.

The other babies seem to know what's going on and avoid the dying one. Yet, when I had three in one small container together and one baby conifer took a turn for the worst and was dying, the other two huddled over it, touched it and stood with it all night long, to give it comfort. They even have empathy at this young age.

This last one, *Surprise*, who was from a batch of six baby conifers, attempted to drink the day before he started to pass. He crawled onto my hand the day of his death and started to lose his footing a tiny bit. He made himself comfortable on my thumbnail and stood still, but started to collapse anyway, losing all of his energy. Earlier that day, I had tried to put water on the end of his drinking straw, but he jumped with fright, as he didn't like the water touching it at all. I felt helpless to save him.

Surprise was approximately a month old and never did the 2nd molt. He had the sweetest, cutest personality. He came into this world with a pure little heart and soul and was so loving. I believe he got it from his parents…. both of who were kind and loving themselves. It is true that good breeds good and evil breeds evil. I have witnessed it in the offspring of both Western Conifer Seed Bugs and Shield bugs.

BUGS THAT LOVE! By Lori-Michele

Notice how small the baby *Surprise* is in comparison to the size of a toothpick in this photo. Also see how small his empty egg case is in the upper left of the picture.

Baby Western conifer Surprise

BUGS THAT LOVE! By Lori-Michele

Very few of the baby conifers will ever make it to adulthood. It was very frustrating and mysterious to see so many of them die and I asked more questions to entomologists to figure out why. I was told that one main reason could be, that because they hatched in the wintertime in my house, there wasn't enough humidity, like there would be outside, in springtime. This made some sense, but it still didn't seem like the answer. After all, how much humidity is in April or May in the Northeast, United States?

I wondered if sugar water simply wasn't enough nutrition or the proper nutrition for these baby conifers. Surely they eat something else, when out in the wild, but what?

I did get some pine nuts at the store and I crushed them up, thinking maybe the oils of the nuts could provide nutrition. Some tasted the oils, but it didn't stop them from dying.

I had to just assume that maybe something genetic caused it. But when they start to pass away, there is nothing you can do to save them. I just tried to give them comfort and touched their little antennae with the end of a toothpick and they have enough intelligence to know that you are there- caring, consoling and trying to help them. I do believe they are comforted by your efforts.

It is amazing that something so tiny, such as these baby conifers, can connect emotionally with something so gigantic in size to them- a human being! They like being with me and love to crawl on my hands and arms and I feel, that they feel safe and well-protected by me. They understand that I'm there to watch out and care for them.

As the others continue to grow and stay strong, you'll notice their little individual personalities and it's adorable! They will go through five molts and it is something to see and very odd at the same time.

The first molt is when they are only between a day and four days

BUGS THAT LOVE! By Lori-Michele

old. It's pretty quick and fast and you most likely will miss it. Instead, you'll just find their old skins left behind and at first think, it's just another little baby bug, but it's really an empty black skin.

Before they molt, they seem to be a little fatter in the couple days before it happens. They do a little antcy dance, moving each leg, stepping up and down and looking very anxious. Then they slow down and don't move as much and finally, they remain still. They know something big is about to happen. Then, they finally get a solid stance and the molting begins.

I have to say, that at first, I found this strange and creepy. To me, it was like watching a sci-fi movie. The molting starts at the back of their head, as their old skin ruptures and splits open all the way down their back, sort of like unzipping a wetsuit. They lift their 'new' emerging head and body, up and back out, as their old skin comes forward. They pull each leg out of their casing and step out, leaving the old skin behind, which is all black and papery. Everything comes out and off, the entire skin of head, back, antennae, drinking straw and legs, to reveal their new and bigger body underneath.

Right after the molt, they look like reddish-pink shrimp with little black eyes. They move their new longer drinking straw up and down, under their bodies, for about 5 minutes.

All of this is pretty much exhausting to them and they settle down and just sit for a long time while they get darker in color, which takes a few hours.

BUGS THAT LOVE! By Lori-Michele

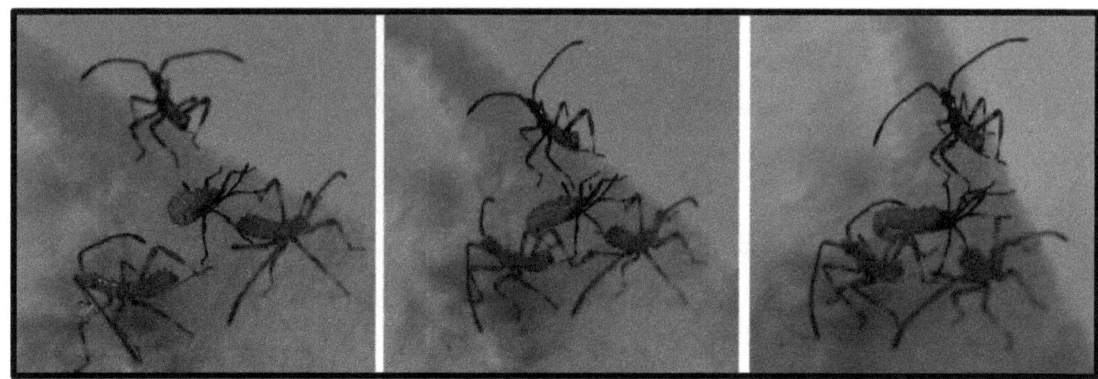

The baby Western conifer, in the center of all these photos, is going through his first molt, as his head emerges up and out of his old exoskeleton, while the others surrounding him have already finished.

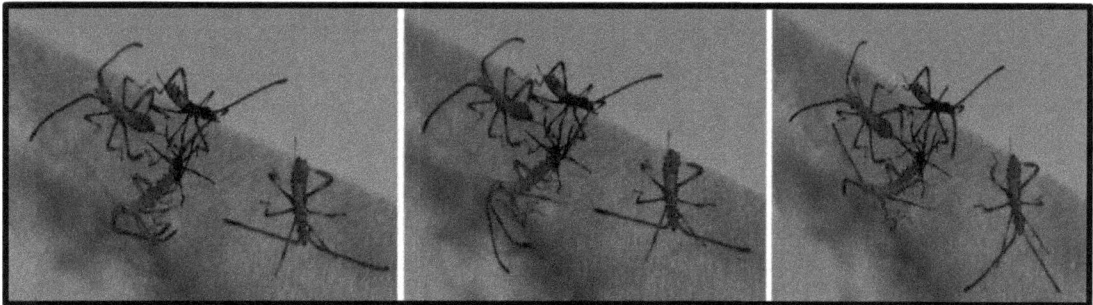

The baby Wester conifer continues to emerge further out of his exoskeleton and leave the skin behind.

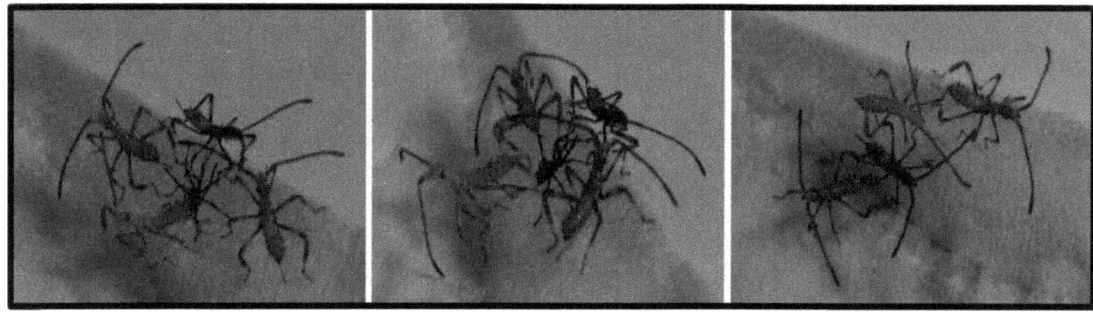

As the baby Western conifer finishes molting, he fully steps out and away from the old black skin; then joins the others, as he too will begin to darken in color, as the time passes. Notice how the one who molted first, (the second one in the photo to the far right), is darker than the rest.

BUGS THAT LOVE! By Lori-Michele

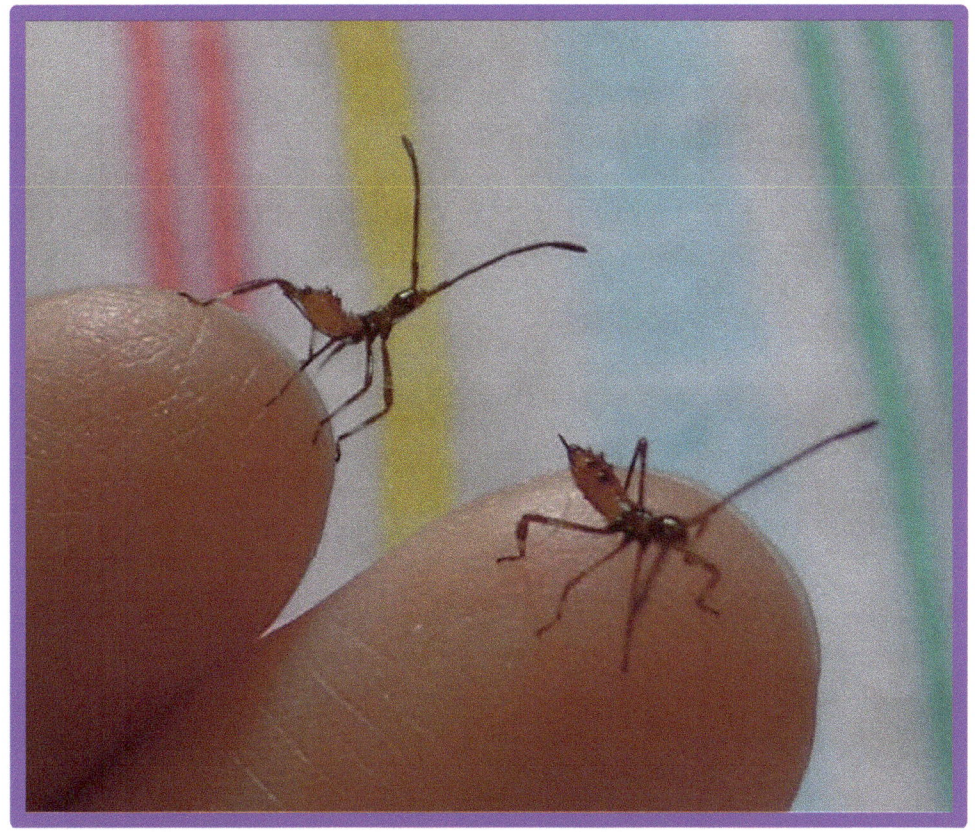

The baby Western conifers a few days later, after molting.

As they get bigger, they will molt four more times, after the initial molt. They only problem is, that at any one of these stages they can die from it. One got stuck in its old skin and couldn't get its head out. Although I tried to assist, it was too hard and difficult to figure out where the old skin and new body began and too risky to tear at any of it.

Others have a difficult time getting their feet out of the skins. I helped this situation a couple of times by putting some water by cotton swab, on the old skin, so it would slip off better.

Yet, another weird thing happens, which is at any of these molting stages, they can be total perfect and fine in one stage and when they molt again, become deformed in the next. For example, one had perfectly normal feel and legs, yet when it molted, it had 'bent knees' and extra long feet. Another one was totally normal before the molting and after, all it's stylets were out of the drinking straw. One of the stylets was short and bent backwards, another was long and wavy, another was curled and the other was bent and twisted. The bug tried endlessly to get them straight and back into the drinking straw, but couldn't. Sometimes, when they are deformed after a molting, they will die soon, yet this one lived for quite a while before it did eventually pass.

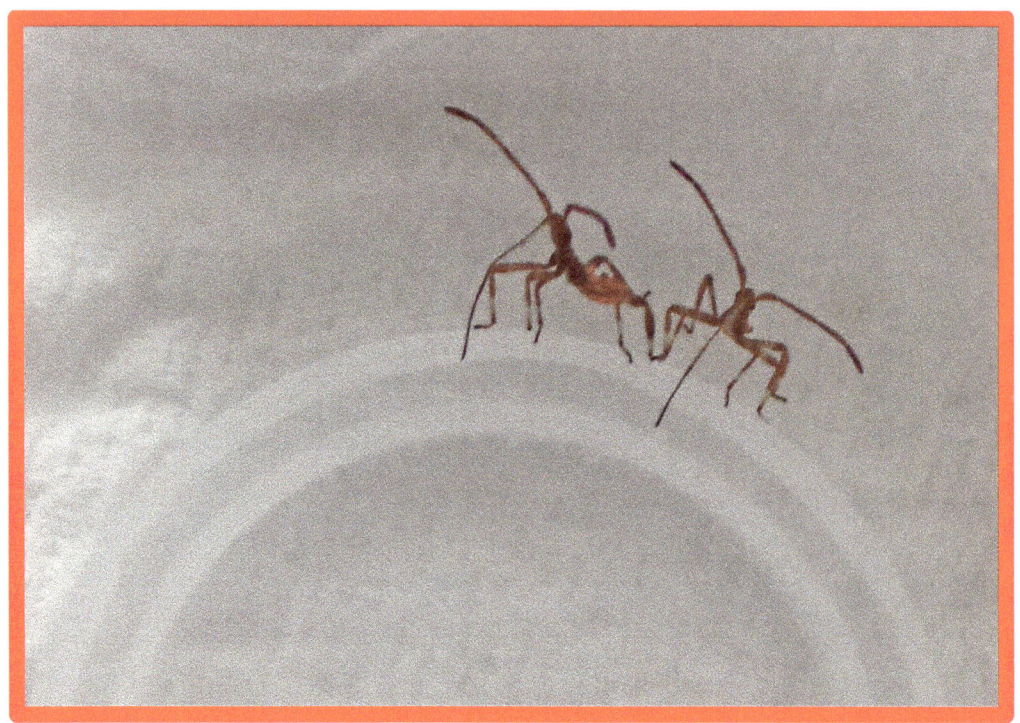

Baby Western conifers at one month old, drinking from a plastic gallon water bottle cap.

I let the young Western conifers crawl all over my computer and many would lay right out on a warmer part of it and stay there for an hour or more. I tried to make sure they didn't stay there for too long, as I didn't want them to 'cook.' I feel that it helped some of the bugs to get to their next stage in molting, from the warm heat, but it didn't work with all of them.

BUGS THAT LOVE! By Lori-Michele

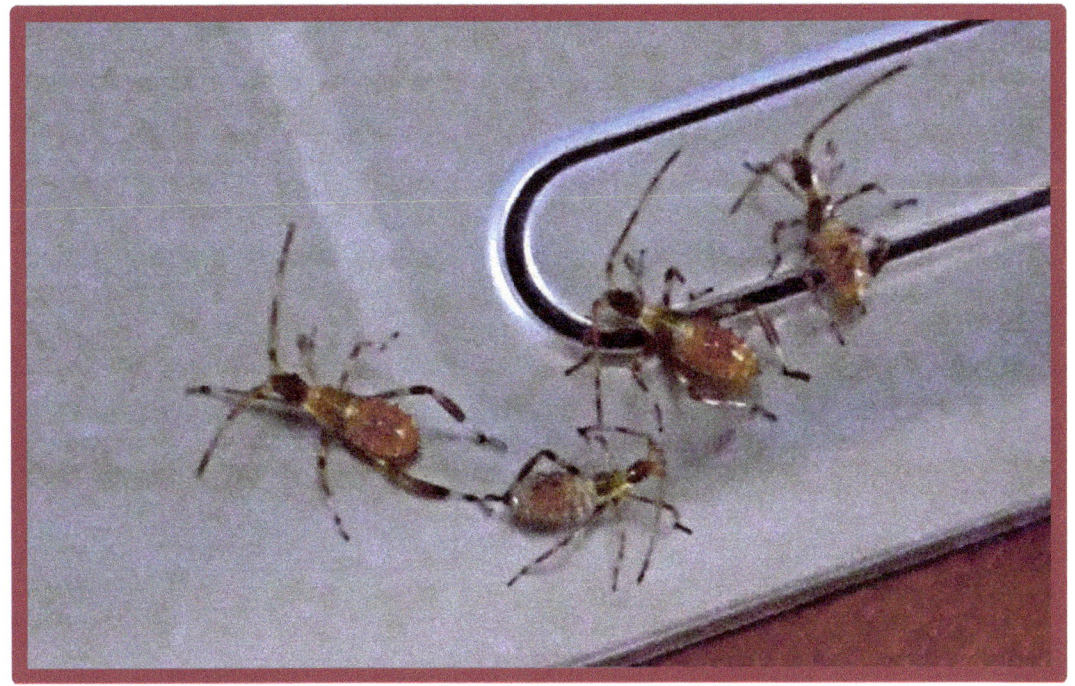

Enjoying the warmth of the computer.

They pretty much stay the same looking for all the molts, as they get bigger and bigger and you find yourself holding your breath and wondering if any will make it to the fifth and final molt. But after the fourth, you'll notice a bit more of a change, as they get plumper and a bit longer and now they stand a good chance of making it to adulthood.

When the final molt happens, it is very long and laborious and completely drains their energy. Again, they are all bright orange-reddish with black eyes and as the hours pass, the full and final colors of the adult pattern on their wings, comes in, as they get darker and darker. It's amazing to witness because during the 4th and 5th molts, you simply don't see the development of their two full sets of wings, both inner and outer, and the intricate pattern on them and it's such a surprise!

BUGS THAT LOVE! By Lori-Michele

Maybe (top in photo) just after her 5th molt. Button who molted earlier that day (bottom in photo) as all his final colors appear.

BUGS THAT LOVE! By Lori-Michele

Here is Maybe, as the pattern comes in on her wings, after her 5th molt.

They are so physically spent, they don't move for a day. But then, the next day or day after that, they will decide to try out their wings and fly a short distance. It's awesome to see them fly… they just automatically know how! Some can exhaust you, as you chase after them, trying to make sure they don't fly and fall into a place where they could get hurt. I had one that flew every chance he could because he was so excited to be able to fly and explore new areas of the house!

BUGS THAT LOVE! By Lori-Michele

CHAPTER 6

MY STORIES ABOUT SOME SPECIAL WESTERN CONIFER SEED BUGS

Here are several stories about some of my special pet conifer bugs and certain things that happened.

The first conifer I ever had as a pet, was named **Buggy**.

One day in December 2011, my father saw a Western conifer on the inside of the storm door and took pity on him. He said "If I leave him there, he'll freeze to death tonight," so he got some newspaper and the little bug readily crawled onto it and Dad brought him into the house.

When he asked later that night, "Did you see that bug I brought in?" I pooh-poohed it and said "What bug?" The next day he asked, "Where did that bug go?" and I just dismissed it.

A few days later, I noticed the bug at the very top of the Christmas tree, crawling on my homemade star topper. Soon, he was on the top of it and I took a picture of him.

Buggy on top of the Christmas tree star & close-up photo.

BUGS THAT LOVE! By Lori-Michele

I had lots of Christmas wrapping paper in a tall, thin basket and I watched him crawling on them, going from roll to roll. I thought he was so cute, but I didn't want to get too attached to him because I didn't know how long he'd live or if he'd suddenly disappear someday, so I just decided to name him Buggy.

He was such an outgoing little thing and I took a liking to him, but I didn't get too close because I didn't know if he was poisonous or would bite. I decided to use a Christmas card to transfer Buggy from place to place and he was leery at first, but then trusting, as he crawled on and off the card.

I gave him some water on the kitchen floor and he drank it. Another time, I gave him sugar in the water and he liked that even more! Then I started to give him sugar water a couple times a day.

Initially, I put yellow food coloring in the water dish because I thought it had to be colored for him to drink it- something he could recognize like outdoor pollen, from a flower. But then I found out that plain sugar water was okay by him and he didn't need the food coloring at all to drink it.

I got the courage one day, on December 30th, to let Buggy crawl onto my finger and it was a thrill! His little feet were so cute, as he gently walked all over my hand, with no fear of me and he was so fascinating to watch. Being very independent, he liked to crawl here and there all day and fly once and a while.

He was brought into the house with an injured back leg, that eventually came off one day and he needed to rest because of it. I felt sorry for him and placed him on a soft potholder and then put it under the Christmas tree. He seemed content to be there and loved the softness of the cloth. He would gravitate to soft things, like Kleenex®, the furniture covers, hand towels, potholders, etc.

Buggy would fly off and crawl wherever he wanted in the house and would disappear from sight for a long while and then

BUGS THAT LOVE! By Lori-Michele

suddenly show up on a chair or table and all other various places.

We decided to use flashlights to walk to the bathroom at night so we wouldn't step on him, if he happened to be on the floor at that time, but he never once wandered at nighttime.

He decided to make a weaved wooden basket (where I kept a plant inside of it) his favorite place to hang out and then to sleep. He liked to crawl up the side of it and onto the top ledge and then spend time grooming himself, cleaning his feet and antennae.

Buggy never liked to be dirty and was bothered by any lint that he would collect on them. He would release some spit, onto his two front feet and then bring down one antenna at a time, patting them from top to midway down and then pull his two front feet down the rest of the length of each antenna, to make them clean. He also rubbed all his other feet together, two at a time, to get all washed up.

I never kept him caged, so I put a small plastic strainer over him when he was crawling on an end table, to keep him safe, whenever I used the vacuum cleaner.

Buggy also liked to crawl up the TV cart, but every time I played the Harry Potter® video game and he'd hear the man's voice blaring from the TV speakers, Buggy would run down the TV cart, across the rug towards me and up my chair, where I'd be sitting. He knew he'd be safe if he was near me, as he learned I was his protector. There was just something that scared him terribly whenever he heard that man's voice and he'd always come running home to me, when that game was playing on the TV.

As the days and weeks passed, I decided to hold him more. He was very relaxed and content in my hands and liked to groom himself. He could stay there forever and was displeased when I'd put him back onto a plant, but would accept it.

BUGS THAT LOVE! By Lori-Michele

He enjoyed being around us and hearing our voices, while we'd be talking about the day, as he crawled around on the leaves of a plant. He'd also listen to the TV whenever there'd be movies on. He adapted and fit in with our lifestyle and became accustomed to it. He went to bed when we'd turn off the lights for the night, in the living room, but he usually got up every morning just before noon.

Buggy knew his name and I'd call out for him over and over and then he'd show up on the carpet, from wherever he was hiding. Sometimes when he got lost for a day or two, he'd be happy to be found and willing to be returned to his familiar basket, as he was now "saved" from a strange area and especially if he was tired and couldn't find his way back! He equated that I was a safe person, who he could trust and that I would take care of him.

He liked to crawl up the wooden poles that supported a tall tree plant and when he got to the top, he'd sit there and look down at everything. I use to look up and say to him, "Buggy, you come down from there!" and soon after, he'd crawl half-way down and then I'd extend my hand and he'd crawl onto it.

Buggy always strived to reach for more, even if it meant falling off the tree plant and into the dirt several feet below. He loved to explore and his nature was to fear at first, but with my encouragement, he'd venture forward.

When I would hold him and walk from one room to another, he'd cling and hang onto my finger tightly, as he would be frightened by the wind and speed. But I would tell him, "It's ok, we're going to the other room," and when I'd sit down again, he'd start to crawl because he knew we weren't traveling anymore. When I did this for the first time though, he got so frightened he peed on my hand, but he never did that again.

One time he was on his end table and I was at the computer table a distance away. Having the ability to recognize me, Buggy decided to venture off and seek me out because he liked being

BUGS THAT LOVE! By Lori-Michele

with me. He figured out that he'd have to crawl down the side of the end table, across the vast kitchen floor, up the leg of my computer table and onto the tablecloth, before he'd arrive at his destination.

Suddenly there he was, before me! He had traveled a great distance to get to where I was, as he didn't fly to get there, but his determination proved successful! Buggy now happily sat on my hand and looked at the computer screen, as I worked. Then he'd eventually crawl onto the computer keyboard, all around on the top of the tablecloth, on and over some books, and then back to me, but he wouldn't leave the area.

Buggy walking on the end table.

When it was bedtime, I would always say to him "It's time to go to bed Buggy. It's bedtime now," and I'd then turn out the light. He would crawl down inside 'his' basket and go to sleep all night until daytime. In the morning, I'd sometimes call to him, "It's time to get up Buggy" and he'd crawl to the top of the basket from inside. Other times, he'd already be up and walking on the top of the ledge, washing up or crawling onto the leaves and stems of the houseplant that was held inside the large basket. Sometimes he would hide under the green pot rim of the houseplant or under the paper plate that was under the plant in the basket and it was so adorable!

Every day was a joy with Buggy. He took a liking to me and would fly to wherever I was, especially in the kitchen and land on my hair, shirt or arm. But one day, on Jan. 21, 2012, an accident occurred.

I was washing the dishes and I felt a tickle on my neck. I just reached up with my gloved hand to swish away the itch and brought my hand down towards the sink.

What I didn't know, was that Buggy had flown onto my neck to be near me and I swept him off and into the sink that was full of hot suds and a few dishes!! As the water continued to pour down from the faucet, I noticed a strange looking thing in the sink that appeared to look like a colorful bumblebee. Without thinking, I grabbed it by the up-righted stiff wings and plucked it out of the suds and put it onto the wet sponge. I realized then, it was Buggy!! I didn't know or had even seen that when Western conifers spread their wings apart, there is a pattern on their back that is similar in color to a bee, with bright yellow and black stripes.

I gently poured some cool water on him, to rinse the suds off and then I placed him on some toilet paper, to wick away and absorb the water quickly. But the strong dish soap and hot water from moments before had done their job. He must have been in shock, because his wings stood up high and stiff, in a frozen position, exposing his striped back and he didn't respond to me or move his body at all. I was convinced that I had accidentally killed him. I talked to him and moved his body back and forth, but it was all rigid. I was sick... what had I done?!! He had flown to me because he wanted to be near me and this is what I did to him?!! I couldn't believe it.

BUGS THAT LOVE! By Lori-Michele

One and a half hours later, when my father came home, I told him the story and he went over and looked at Buggy, who was still in that frozen position, with his wings held up high. I placed him in his hand and my father moved him back and forth, just as I had done, but miraculously, he moved a bit and suddenly he lowered his wings down to the normal position. Oh my God… he was alive!! How could that be???

Buggy had his drinking straw half bent and sticking out and he slowly put it under himself. Later, he was rocking his body back and forth and put his little front foot forward, in an attempt to get back to his normal self, but his body wasn't ready yet.

I spent enormous sums of time with him and encouraged him that I was there. He was so weak and I thought he'd never want to go near water again, especially after what I did to him, but he wanted to drink and I feel he was trying to get better. I got some toilet paper and soaked it with some sugar water and I assisted him as he tried, ever so slowly, to pull his drinking straw forward and he drank the sugar water. He continued to be weak and all his legs were useless. It was as if he had some type of stroke.

I worried about him all night and checked on him a few times and he had moved position twice. When I got up in the morning, he didn't want to drink and instead just wanted to be held.

Buggy finally drank for 3 minutes off a cotton swab that I soaked in sugar water and then he tried to walk as usual, but was very shaky. I calmed him down so he wouldn't push himself so hard to return to normal too quickly. He rested on the toilet paper I placed him on and an hour later he tried to clean his antennae, but he couldn't bring them down. Instead he tried to bring his two front feet together to pat, but the antenna wasn't there, so he was patting the air. He was still doing the gesture though. His whole body was leaning to the right side, but he was trying very hard to return to who he was before the accident.

Day after day, he got a little stronger, but when he tried to crawl, he had some kind of damage that he couldn't move his legs well at all. He was shaking, like an old man with a cane. He'd raise his front leg up to take a step forward and it would shake all over and then he would place it down. His other legs were the same. This lasted for a long time and we thought he'd be disabled like this from now on…. that somehow, the accident damaged him permanently.

We tried to give him pomegranate juice, but it was too strong. Then we gave him a grape from some canned fruit cocktail and he loved that!

He was determined to go on with his life and as the days passed, he got better and better and we couldn't believe what we were seeing. He was recovering from the damage and his weakness and shakiness were slowly disappearing and he was walking smoother and stronger, until he returned to his normal self! He was finally able to control and bring down his antennae and clean them perfectly, as he had before the accident.

By January 26th, he seemed back to normal, returning to his former self and crawling up his basket, like he always did. The next day, he walked a lot all over the houseplants, for the first time since his accident and he had appeared to make a full recovery. I gave him a combination of pear juice and sugar water to try and he drank for fifteen minutes. He then slept in my hand for a while and I gently put him back onto his basket.

Two weeks later, on Feb. 11th, he was the same as ever. He had crawled a lot that day and he rested on my hand for an hour, as I watched TV. But just after 5 pm., he suddenly started to shake all over, took a couple steps forward and then his legs collapsed under him all at once. I was shocked, upset and confused. If he had done so well in returning to his former self and recovered fully from the accident, then why did this happened?!

The next hours were terrible. He was totally weak, as I tried to prop his feet up and even tried to get him to drink from the Q-tip®, but his antennae were limp and went down. His legs were

BUGS THAT LOVE! By Lori-Michele

flattened, but his feet were stiff. We felt he had some sort of seizure and was now dying.

We never thought we could get so close to a bug and come to love it. We had an emotional bond with him because he knew and trusted us. He adapted easily and learned. He recognized it was me, whenever I excitedly shouted "Buggy, Buggy" or lovingly spoke and said, "a bug-a-bug," into his antennae and he always raised his antennae when we spoke to him. He loved to be held and talked to and even sung to. If he didn't want to get off my finger, then he'd turn his body around and stay there. He'd scratch his eye with his feet, if he had an itch and he'd use his hind legs to scratch the back of his wing or use a middle leg to scratch a hind leg. Sometimes, I'd gently blow air on his back and he'd open and raise his wings to reveal his striped black and yellow back and then he'd scratch his wings again. He had a memory of color and hated the color red.

His determination to overcome always pulled him through. He overcame the loss of his leg and then his devastating sink accident and stroke-like after effects. When he regained his strength, he even tried to fly again, but could only hop-fly along.

In his short life, he suffered, fought, endured and triumphed.

We never knew a bug had so many emotions, feelings, a memory and intelligence. He was so caring and loving and he had such a vibrant personality. He could translate vocal human tones of speech to understand, learn and adapt.

Buggy was such an affectionate bug and taught us so much in the two months he was with us. We even learned that something in him had the ability to repair something similar to a stroke and a Parkinson's-type shake to full recovery, after he had his traumatic, near-death accident in the sink and that these bugs most likely could have the answers to human health problems and diseases.

….And we never thought that we could hurt so bad and cry so

BUGS THAT LOVE! By Lori-Michele

much with his death, at the loss of his cute little personality and all that he was because he was so special!

Tina was a very independent female conifer. She wasn't caged and loved to climb up the living room drape and crawl on the top of the curtain rod. But she was also, amazingly loving.

When my father got sick with a bad cold, in early 2013, he rested on the daybed in an alcove of the living room. Tina would watch over him and crawl to the furthest side of the curtain rod and stare down at him for hours, while he coughed and suffered. When the lights went out at night, she'd go and hide on the backside of the curtains. In the morning she'd be crawling on the top of the curtain rod again. But every night, she'd walk over to the far end of the curtain rod, on top of the drapes and just stare over and look down at my father, while he continued to have his cold night after night.

Tina somehow knew he was sick and wasn't himself and she stood there watching over him for hours, instead of crawling everywhere like she always did, in her usual daily routine. Her understanding of the situation and compassion were amazing to see.

Tina drinking at the water dish.

BUGS THAT LOVE! By Lori-Michele

Autumn got her name because she came to the front door, on the second day of autumn. She was an incredibly special and intelligent Western conifer. She had a temperament that was always calm, classy and sophisticated and she took everything in stride, never overreacting to anything.

When she arrived on the front door, that chilly day, she simply stood put on the outside door frame. Dad ignored her and left to do an errand, but when he got back, she was still on the door frame, patiently waiting. Then we went for a walk and when we got back, she was still there. She had a missing back right leg, but it didn't seem to bother or affect her in any way. I held my finger up to the front of her face and she calmly reached out a foot and then another to climb aboard, with no fear or caution at all. She totally trusted me and I happily brought her into the warm house.

I made a little cage to keep her safe at nighttime and gave her a cap of sugar water. During the day, she liked to fly to the ceiling lamp and do several laps around it. Then I'd call out to her and hold my hands up high towards and under the ceiling lamp and just stand there waiting, until she was finished doing her 'laps' and then she'd fly down, landing on my hand, wrist or arm sleeve. I'd sit down and tell her she was "a good girl." She'd then fly off and back up and around the ceiling lamp again and return to land on my hand once more. This was both a form of exercise for her and a fun game.

Soon, other Western conifers came and I took them into the house as well. I decided to put two other conifers in the cage with Autumn and I got a big cloth for the other three to hide in and stay warm, that I just left next to the screened cage on the table.

Autumn was the only one with a missing back right leg, but the temperaments of the others concerned me. She didn't take to them well and they didn't take to her either. She was the classy, sophisticated one and they were all wild and rambunctious.

BUGS THAT LOVE! By Lori-Michele

Autumn when she first arrived.

One morning, on Nov. 5th, 2013, I got up and went to open the living room drape, as I always did, but first, I looked into the cage and thought I saw Autumn and the two others. I assumed that the three conifers were asleep in the large, soft cloth, next to the cage. But what I didn't know was that Betsy (who we found out the next day was really a large-sized male we renamed Biggy), had climbed out of the cloth and somehow snuck under the bottom of the screening and into the cage, where I safely kept Autumn.

Autumn, who had never escaped or wandered before, must have been frightened of Biggy when he entered and so she climbed out from under the cage to escape and somehow wound up on the carpeted floor!

I never had a reason to look down on the carpet, as I thought all

BUGS THAT LOVE! By Lori-Michele

the conifers were safe and sleeping in their beds, as I opened the living room drape. I unknowingly damaged Autumn's entire left side with one of my slippers and walked away.

When I returned to the room, I spotted her crawling as fast as she could on the carpet towards me and I bent down and picked her up right away. I assessed quickly what happened, as I looked into the cage and saw Biggy, who was the missing conifer from the cloth and then I examined Autumn.

Her back left leg was torn off and both the middle and front one were badly injured. Yet, she thought I had come to her rescue and was trying to comfort her! She didn't know it was me who did such a terrible, yet unintentional thing to her. I felt so incredibly guilty and I comforted her all day, hoping she'd live through this awful accident.

At this time, and fairly new to Western Conifer Seed Bugs, I believed that all the bugs I had brought into the house were all females and I didn't have a reason to believe there was a male in the group. But, the very next morning, I found Biggy mating with her and that's when I found out he was a male! I isolated him in his own cage.

Now poor Autumn not only had to re-cooperate from her bad accident, but she would also have to lay eggs!

As the days passed, Autumn's left front leg came off and her middle leg stiffened straight, but wouldn't detach. She hobbled around, but never had any show of sorrow, misery or defeat. She struggled to crawl around with dogged determination and she even pulled herself up, on the inside of the screened cage and climbed all the way to the top of it, with only two working legs on the right side because it was one of her favorite things to do. If she fell off, she'd just continue to crawl back up again! I found her twice, upside down, kicking her remaining legs in the air. There was no way for her to right herself, so I'd just put my finger over the waving legs and she'd grab on and I'd put her back right-side up.

BUGS THAT LOVE! By Lori-Michele

On the 19th of November, she laid 5 eggs. A low number, but since she was so injured, it's amazing she laid eggs at all.

Autumn always persevered, no matter what happened. She longed to be normal, despite being so damaged.

She knew and recognized that the round yellow lid was the place to get a drink of water. Initially, she could only lie sideways and used her right front foot to grab onto the side of the water dish and put her drinking straw up, over and into the sugar water. Later, I got a plastic fork that held her body up securely and then placed it into the low-level water, so she could dip her drinking straw in-between the tongs, to drink more comfortably.

She desperately yearned to groom herself, like she did before the accident, so I assisted her by physically holding up the left side of her body just high enough, for her to spit on and wet her two feet, so she'd be able to clean her antennae. Sometimes she acted as if she still had the left foot and I believe she thought she's was cleaning the left antenna that she lowered to do so, as she moved her right foot very, very fast against it, although she really needed the other foot to do the cleaning properly. She always took such pride in keeping herself clean, more than any other conifer I ever had.

Autumn always enjoyed sitting in my warm hand or pulling herself up the side of my index finger and resting her right front leg over it, to look around and watch everything. She wanted to take it all in and be a part of it. She had such an inquisitive nature and enjoyed sitting on the arm of the sofa chair, so she could watch me and see everything that was going on in the room, in all directions.

Many times Autumn just wanted to crawl like she did before and she would, only now it was such a struggle, but she never stopped trying. She would just pull herself forward, with her front and second leg and sometimes would go in a circle. The left leg stump would get stuck or caught on the sofa chair fabric or even on the inside of the screened cage sometimes, but she just kept tugging and pulling, until she got to where she wanted to go. The middle left stiffened leg sometimes acted as a balance for her, on that left side, which was helpful.

One day, she showed me through body language the discomfort she was in, as she was trying to open her upper shoulders, to get her wings apart. They were stuck together because some sugar water had gotten on them and hardened. I assisted her with a toothpick, to get her wings apart, and she knew what I was trying to do and offered me some of her spittle from the end of her drinking straw, thinking that if she gave me some of her spit, it would help and work. No bug before or after her ever did that and I was completely amazed and touched, that she was trying to help me, to help her.

I used some warm water on a Q-tip® to soak her sugar-stuck wings, along with the toothpick and also blew on her back, as we worked together. She was finally able to slowly pull them apart and then held her wings open and up for me, as I worked on the second pair underneath. Autumn was very happy when we were successful in getting them all free and moveable again, so she'd feel normal once more.

She never overexerted and made sure to take little naps and rest and then go on her merry way. She loved to watch TV and liked the music I played on the radio and when I sung to her.

Autumn would sometimes tell me when she was thirsty, by holding out her drinking straw. Then I'd get the plastic fork and she'd readily climb quickly onto it, pulling herself forward. When I lowered her on the fork, into the low level sugar water, she'd put her drinking straw into the water right away and drink for a half to one hour. Sometimes when I'd place her on the fork and into the sugar water, if she didn't want a drink, she'd just sit there patiently until I took her out. (Please note that she wasn't submerged in the water at all.)

Meanwhile, Biggy had earlier mated with another female conifer and she laid eggs as well. When one of the eggs hatched, the

BUGS THAT LOVE! By Lori-Michele

little baby named Filbert, walked over to Autumn. It playfully crawled onto her antenna, while she was on the fork, drinking. Autumn naturally, with maternal instinct, gently lifted him up high into the air with her antenna and down towards her back, and waited for him to crawl off, which he did!

Autumn with another female Western conifer's baby Filbert, on her drinking fork.

On Dec. 5th, Autumn's eggs also started to hatch and one I named Chrissy (for Christmas). She was a bright, ready-to-go, sassy little thing, who began running all over the place right away. Autumn didn't much care it was hers or pay any attention to her. Chrissy almost drown in some water and it changed her wild behavior, as she wasn't charging and so gutsy anymore. It seems that little ones do learn from their accidents.

On Dec. 12th, Autumn's stiff middle leg broke off and now she didn't have any legs on the left side, which made crawling and drinking more difficult, as there wasn't anything to support and balance her on that side anymore. Still, she determinedly pulled herself forward, struggling along, to crawl. I noticed it tired her immensely and she would just stop and rest. She also slept more.

Caring for this pet bug wasn't too hard, just a little more effort was needed. And since she had such a loving personality and human-like emotions, I gave her all the attention I could. She thought of herself as equal to all the others or even better and wanted to keep up with them, no matter what. She wanted to be active and crawl and she did so, just with so much more effort. And even after she lost all the legs on her left side, she still never gave up her pride and love of grooming.

Autumn adapted to the missing legs. Using ingenuity, she eventually found a way to clean her antennae herself. It all started that she crawled up the inside of the screened cage and lost her footing one day, but held on with one leg- the right middle one. As she swung backward, her back was suddenly supported by the screen and she figured that she could use her free front right foot to clean her antennae. Then, she found a way to do this on her bed roll, by hanging off the end, open part of the roll with the middle leg and cleaning with the front foot. She also used her spittle, to wet her foot as well! Any way that she could clean those antennae, was the very most important thing to her!

She continued to stay as active as she could, crawling on the bed roll, the screened cage and the paper floor, along with the others. She wanted to be and feel normal and keep up with the rest of the female conifers. They knew she was permanently injured and sometimes they would come over and just sit with her or they'd touch antennae or drink together.

BUGS THAT LOVE! By Lori-Michele

Autumn (center) drinking with her friends.

She refused to be 'a cripple' and didn't want to be treated as so. She didn't like things done for her, she wanted to do them herself. And she was fiercely independent. She went to bed when she wanted to and got up when she wanted, whether that was early or late; she found new ways to clean her antennae; she'd play on her cloth bed roll or pine clippings; sometimes she'd just sit and stare most of the day; and she loved to sit high up on her bed roll and listen to and watch TV with her antennae held high, being very alert, as we watched movies. She also liked to be involved with whatever was happening during the day and at nighttime, she'd love to be perched up and over, on my hand, with intense interest in watching TV.

BUGS THAT LOVE! By Lori-Michele

Autumn perched on my hand to look over and watch TV.

Another amazing thing is that she learned how to be moved, by me using a toothpick. I'd place it in front of her and she'd grab it with her front right foot and grip it tightly, as I said, "Okay, we're gonna go now," and I'd lift her up in the air with it and then I'd gently lower her down into the palm of my hand or onto her cloth bed roll or wherever I wanted to move her. She never let go while being carried and then she'd release her grip when she knew she was in my hand or on cloth, etc. She was so very adept at this and never forgot that this was used to move her around. She also learned on her own, that if she didn't want to be moved, she would simply let her foot be loose and let it slip off the toothpick and not grip it. It was her way of saying "I don't want to go from where I am."

Autumn had been moody for a few days, acting oddly and

BUGS THAT LOVE! By Lori-Michele

seeming very agitated. Then, she became her normal self again. I found 19 eggs, laid in a chain line, in her bed roll and that explained her behavior. Only 4 of the eggs looked like something was in them. I was told by entomologists that sometimes they just lay empty eggs, to get rid of them. The fertile ones were from when she mated three months ago, as they sometimes store the sperm inside their bodies and lay more eggs later. Surprisingly, those four eggs hatched. Only one of her babies made it to adulthood and his name was *Button*.

Close-up of empty egg cases. Notice the built-in escape hatch, that is circular on every egg case.

One day, Autumn was crawling around in her cage and stopped in the middle of the white paper floor between two bed rolls and she looked bored. She was just sitting there, her view basically nothing, blocked by the cloths. I bent down, at the side of the cage and I called and started to talk to her and she raised her antennae up and turned her head slightly and then she finally saw me. She got excited, then started to turn herself in my direction and crawl over towards me. She could hear me, knew me, recognized me and wanted to be near me and communicate

BUGS THAT LOVE! By Lori-Michele

with me. I tried this several times, when she'd be looking off in another direction and the reaction was always the same.

I was told by entomologists that the Western conifers don't see like we do, but Autumn always recognized me. I was told they don't hear like we do, but every time I spoke to Autumn, she'd raise her antennae and move toward me. I was told, bugs don't sleep, but they do, as they put their antennae down and outward while they sleep. And they also don't believe that these bugs can communicate with you or try to do so, but that is so untrue.

Every time I held Autumn in my hand and carried her around, when I spoke to her, she'd signal back to me, that she heard me and would communicate back an acknowledgement, by lifting her front or middle leg up and then tapping it down a few times. She understood and wanted to talk with me, but couldn't and this was her way of communicating to me, that she did in fact hear and understand me and was talking back, through physical gestures.

Autumn loving to be held and carried around.

BUGS THAT LOVE! By Lori-Michele

She loved to be cozy in her warm, cloth bed roll, in the winter months, all the way through March. She would crawl inside, but leave her antennae sticking out, so she could still hear us, yet have the cloth wrapped all around her.

Autumn happy and cozy in her cloth bed roll.

In April, I gave her some fresh pine clippings and she happily drank some sap from them. She was the type that got bored quickly, so when I put the pine clippings in her cage, she thoroughly enjoyed crawling on them to play.

She also loved to be held and would get upset when I set her back down on her bed roll, but I only had so much stamina.

One time, I was talking to her about a half a foot away, as she was hanging out on the end of her bed roll. As she hung onto the cloth with her mid-right leg, she waved her front foot to me in the air over and over, to get my attention, so I'd pick her up! I couldn't believe it! I put my finger over her, as she grabbed on quickly, since she was upside-down and she was happy as a lark to be once again held in my hand.

Then on May 24th, 2014 another bad accident happened, that ultimately lead to her death. My father was carrying her around and she lost her grip on his smooth palm, rolling off and falling about three feet onto the hard kitchen floor. We didn't know it at the time, but it cracked her labium (the drinking straw).

Suddenly, I observed that she seemed to be spending a huge amount of time cleaning, but then after two days of this, I looked closer and noticed that the black stylets had come out of her drinking straw and she was working endlessly to get them back in, so she could drink.

I didn't know what was happening and consulted the entomologists again, who told me what had happened and how the stylets work and that there was no hope for her. My father was extremely guilt-ridden for causing this to happen.

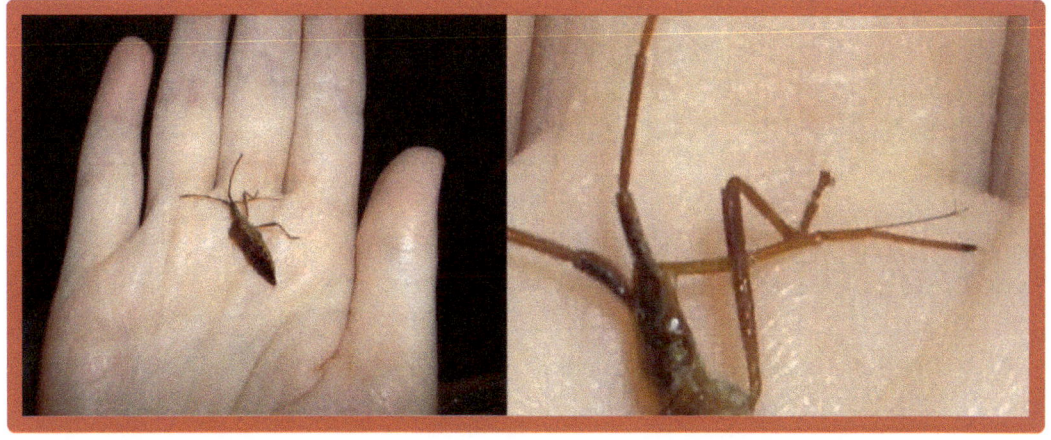

Autumn showing me the problem and close-up view of black, hair-like stylets out of labium (drinking straw) before unraveling to 4 loose strands.

BUGS THAT LOVE! By Lori-Michele

I continued to help Autumn put the drinking straw and the stylets, which appear like thin, black, hair-like threads, into the sugar water, hoping she could somehow get water in them and get some liquid into her. One of the stylets still appeared to work and it could jut in and out, but I didn't know if that would help her or not. She tried to help herself as always and would let them sit in the water for three hours. She knew something was wrong with her, but she never gave up trying to fix herself.

I crushed up some pine nuts and let her rub the stylets into the liquid of them. I hoped she would be able to get some nutrients of the nuts into her via those stylets.

After the accident, she lost all interest in crawling on the inside of the screened cage anymore. She couldn't eat pine nuts, stab the pine clippings or drink normally. She didn't want to go on top of her bed roll and look out at everything anymore either. She didn't clean her antennae or get up early or try to walk over to the water dish and get a drink by herself. She lost all interest in TV. She'd work on trying to get the stylets back into the drinking straw until exhaustion and she'd get depressed and rest. She'd fall asleep in my hand. She started to get darker in color, look old, worried, tired and appeared to lose her abdomen plumpness. She seemed to be trying to survive and conserve her energy, so she didn't crawl much and just slept a lot. She had lost her happy little independent self.

My heart was broken. I couldn't fix her or save her. I just had to try and help her drink and be with her. I'd carry her around and she'd get panicked suddenly and start tapping her foot up and down rapidly in my palm, until I told her it was ok. Then she'd stop moving her foot because I gave her reassurance and she'd rest. She continued to raise her antennae whenever I'd call her name and talk to her.

In the morning, she'd extend her drinking straw to tell me she needed a drink and I'd assist her to put it into the water, along with the loose stylets. At other times, she held it up towards me to show me she had a problem and wanted my help.

BUGS THAT LOVE! By Lori-Michele

I continued to consult entomologists for help in fixing her. I was told by one at Cornell University that if I put her in the refrigerator for ten minutes, it might immobilize her enough, where I could then push the stylets back into the labium tube with tweezers. He said he had no idea if there were any other muscular structures or other tissue structures that held the stylets in the sheath or if they would come out again. But, I simply could not do this to her. I did not have tweezers small enough for this and the structure is more complicated than just simply stuffing the tiny, thin hair-like stylets back in.

Between June 3rd-10th, Autumn had many different behaviors. She acted normally one day and sat on her bed roll with antennae held up high and observed the world around her. But then, she started to sleep more and appear weaker, as her antennae began hanging down. She didn't want to drink because she found it frustrating. Sometimes she would 'lick' the pine nut juice off my hand by moving the stylets in the oil. She would let her foot slip off the toothpick more, as she didn't want to be lifted or moved. She still liked being in 'Mommy's hand' best and I loved that when I talked to her, she'd signal back to me, by moving her second leg.

On June 10th, she crawled out of her bed and rested her head on the pine clippings. I got her to 'drink' for 20 minutes. She still tried to get her stylets back into the drinking straw, but her antennae kept going down, as she was losing strength. By the end of the night she looked weak. She still clung tightly onto the toothpick with both feet, as I lifted her up and into my hand.

On June 12, 2014, I decided to get Autumn up at 11:45 am, but she didn't respond when I lightly blew down the tunnel of the bed roll. She always raised her antennae when I did this because she knew it was me. I opened the cloth and she wasn't responsive.

I placed her into my hands and she was stiff and her antennae were lying down. She moved for me when I talked, always trying no matter what. She knew she was dying, but she fought all the

BUGS THAT LOVE! By Lori-Michele

way to stay here.

At 12:05 pm she moved her head up and down and out, every minute or so. I continually talked to her and said all my special phrases just for her.

At 3:15 pm she stood up in my hand and put her antennae back, but I wondered if she was in pain or not. She flinched and kicked her middle leg and foot a lot.

At 5:15 p.m., as I carried her around in my hand, she raised her antennae up, when I put some laundry on a hanger and into my closet. It seemed to be with curiosity and she wanted to see what I was doing and what was going on.

Most of the time her antennae were down and flat, as she had no strength. I got desperate and took the last pine nuts and squashed them and used the toothpick to rub some oil on her stylets. She seemed to get less shakes, after I did this. She knew I was trying to help her and let me raise up her side to do so.

I even got plain water and applied some of it to the stylets and she put up with me again, hoping that she'd get better.

She lifted her antennae when I called her name and that made me feel better, since she was getting loose and weaker now.

She made it through the whole day and fought like hell. At 9 pm she was succumbing. She was all tired out and resting in my hand, as I put a movie on, like any other day.

At 9:15 pm she raised her left antenna up and back towards me, as I praised her and talked to her and said the name I called her often- "Autumn baby" and told that she was "a good girl."

Later at 10 pm, I went to lift her from underneath with the toothpick and she raised both antennae a bit as if to say, "Hey what's going on, I'm resting here!"

BUGS THAT LOVE! By Lori-Michele

By 11 pm, I believe she had died and it was best that she passed away in 'Mommy's hand' where she knew she was safe and protected and could rest.

I put her onto her bed roll, like I did every night of her life- just as if we were all getting ready for bed. I told her "you're such a good girl, yes you are!" and called her "Autumn baby" again and said "nighty-night" and "mama loves you."

The emotional pain and loss was unbearable. I had grown so close to her and she was much too intelligent to just be a bug. She loved me and I loved her. She always responded when I called her name because she knew her name and would raise her antennae and head up towards me to look at me. She didn't want to die and fought it all day, when other conifers succumb in an hour or two.

I loved talking to her and taking care of her. She loved to be with me and felt safe. She brought us happiness and we did the same for her. She always found life to be fascinating and always wanted to be a part of everything. She was attentive, inquisitive, interested, and wanted to see all and observe. She was never a dumb, mindless bug, who just goes on their way and is oblivious to all. She had a strong, outstanding will and never showed that she was sorry for herself or couldn't do and be as other conifers, even though she had so much against her. She always kept going and I admired her for that especially. She outlived every Western conifer I brought in, even though she had the accident that I naively caused and felt horrible guilt over, that took her three legs and she was left with only two. Forever I will love and miss her. She was just so special and extraordinary.

Applejacks was an adorable male conifer. He loved to be held, all the time! He also liked to crawl up my arm to the top of my shoulder and then across my upper back to the other shoulder and down the other arm. He wouldn't venture too far out of my vision and he liked playing with my hair. He even attempted to crawl up it and he got to the top of my head several times and most conifers don't like dealing with hair at all!

BUGS THAT LOVE! By Lori-Michele

Applejacks happily sitting on the top of my head.

Every morning he'd be waiting for me to put the fresh cap of sugar water down on the floor of his container, so he could walk over to it and get his breakfast. Then he'd rest for an hour and begin to walk around.

I kept two Shield bugs in the container with him, for companions. Applejacks was a true follower and team player. If the Shield bugs were hiding under the cloth bed roll, he'd walk all around and want to be out of his container and with me because he didn't see them anywhere. But if he did see them, he'd mimic their behavior, which was usually slower. Suddenly, he'd be sitting quietly next to them and if they'd sleep, he would too! If they got a drink from the cap, he would copy them!

He would stare at me from inside his container, that I kept next to my computer and when I took him out, he would be totally at home and at peace, just hanging out with me for hours! He just loved companionship!

Applejacks learned and understood routine. When I turned the bright lights out in the living room and kept a dimmer one on, at

BUGS THAT LOVE! By Lori-Michele

nighttime, he knew that meant he had to calm down, before going to bed. He enjoyed me just holding him for an hour, while I watched TV and he'd snuggle into my hand, like a 'lap dog' and just be perfectly content to stay there, to be with me. He'd also rest on the back of my hand sometimes. I had never had a conifer, so able-bodied to just get up and walk or fly away, but instead chose to stay still, stretching his legs out in comfort, while being so peacefully content, for such a long time.

Applejacks resting on the back of my hand.

Then after an hour, he would 'wash-up' his antennae, to get ready for bed. (Western conifers sometimes do this, just as us humans brush our teeth, before we retire for the night.) I'd lower him into his container while he was on my finger and he willingly would step off and onto his cloth bed. He enjoyed spending time with me and was now ready for a good night's sleep.

BUGS THAT LOVE! By Lori-Michele

It's hard to express all the different things he did, but Applejacks had a wonderful, loving, kind temperament and was an adorable pet!

Courage was a special bug from the beginning. We were moving things out of a storage unit on October 29, 2019 and he was on the underside of a box, but we didn't know it. When the box was placed down on top of another box in the trunk of the car, he was caught in-between and I noticed two little antennae waving all around, as if to say, "Hey I'm right here, don't you see me!" We quickly removed the upper box off him, but it was a little late, as he had been damaged by the weight of it.

I held him in my hands and he just exuded such a loving, cute personality, that I decided to take him home. If he was going to pass, I'd make sure he'd do so on soft toilet paper, with me touching and talking to him, to give him comfort and love at home.

This was the first bug that I've had who was injured in this sort of way, that his middle legs actually worked, while the back legs barely did. Usually when they are this damaged and weak, they don't have physical control of the front or middle legs. He already had a missing right front leg, but it appeared that his left front one was damaged with limited movement.

When I did get home, I decided to try and give him a drink. To my surprise, he tried to drink the sugar water I gave him, as I propped him up on the side of the drinking cap. I figured, based on other conifers who had been similarly injured, that he'd be lucky to live a day or two. I hoped beyond hope that he'd live to Halloween. Miraculously, he did live to Halloween and beyond that, although his way of life was different from any other conifer I've had.

We got into a steady routine, since he was such a part of my daily life and he got his name from his determination to live. Courage would be awake in his container around 9 am or earlier and I could tell he was ready to get up and start the day because

BUGS THAT LOVE! By Lori-Michele

his antennae would be raised up high. Then I'd take him out of his container and set him up on his drinking cap and he'd willingly start drinking the sugar water slowly all day. I placed him right next to my computer, so I could talk to and encourage him, as he'd try to drink and he became my little companion.

Courage propped up to drink all day.

His drinking straw appeared like others before him who were injured, where it starts to get darker on the tip, which is another way their bodies shut down, before they die, preventing them from drinking. I can only guess that this is a constriction on the end tip. But he persevered more than the others before him and never gave up trying! For 12 hours a day, he'd try to drink.

Every night, at 9 pm, I'd take him off his drinking cap and hold him. Then I'd sit him down in front of the computer screen, as he loved the moving pictures! I'd play TV shows and movies and he'd watch with his antennae held high and be enthralled at the action on the screen! He even turned his head a bit to look at

BUGS THAT LOVE! By Lori-Michele

everything and he could watch for hours! Sometimes he'd be so involved in a show, I didn't have the heart to turn it off and I'd let him watch till 11:30 pm and even midnight, before I'd put him to bed. I've never had a conifer love TV so much!!

Courage watching a TV movie on the computer screen.

The days passed and then weeks and everyday I'd be surprised and thankful that he was still alive, as I prayed that he'd live another day or longer. How I wanted him to be fully healed because he was so intelligent and loving. After a week or two, he did a little pee on his toilet paper and that was a good sign. Somehow he was getting a tiny bit of liquid in him to survive and keep living.

His front left leg that was injured and that he used to balance with, eventually got bent, twisted and fell off. He was a bit

BUGS THAT LOVE! By Lori-Michele

relieved to be rid of it, as it didn't function properly and then it was just in his way, for a short while.

Also, he, like other male bugs who are injured and dying, had his appendage out and my father believes that when they do that, it's indicative of some sort of fever, when they are badly injured. With Courage, he could have the appendage out for a few days and then it would go back in for a couple days and then it would be out again. It was like he was fighting illness, that he was winning sometimes and losing other times. (Near the end of his life, it went back in again.)

He made it to Thanksgiving and then we put the Christmas tree up on Dec. 5th and played Christmas music. But, he started to get weaker and desperate to give him nutrients to help him, I gave him some cranberry punch to drink. It seemed to perk him up a little bit and he liked the taste of it, as he moved his drinking straw around in it. I did this for a few days, alternating the punch drink for a few hours and then the sugar water as well. But it didn't work as well as I hoped, and soon he wasn't able to drink anymore, although he tried endlessly and never gave up. His legs got weaker and he could barely move them. Then he got so weak, that as I tried to help him with his drinking straw one day and he tried to pull it forward for me a tiny bit, I realized that it would be too much for him and fruitless to have him try and drink all day, when he simply couldn't anymore.

The tips of his antennae had gotten darker, as had his body for the past several days. I let him rest comfortably and pet him and talked to him all day, as he just couldn't give anymore to survive. But amazingly, he did. His will was so strong to keep fighting on, that he didn't pass away quickly.

This is often harder on me than the Western conifer itself, as I want their suffering to end quickly and I am pained a great deal that some do hang on for a while. Day by day passed, but he still responded to me, when I touched and talked to him. At first he would move a leg a small bit and when he could no longer do that, then he would raise his right antenna when I talked to him.

BUGS THAT LOVE! By Lori-Michele

As he got weaker, if I raised an antenna with a toothpick, he'd hold it up for a while before he'd gently lower it again. Such willpower, strength and determination to survive and endless Courage!

I didn't think he'd live more than 2 days and he lived a little longer than 6 weeks. When he could no longer drink, he lasted 5 days before he passed, longer than any other conifer I've had. He was remarkable!

Sweetie Pea was a special Western conifer, who had such reasoning and tolerance. You can always tell when one of these Western conifers has extra intelligence and a special personality.

One day, I had taken her out of her container, despite that I had a very bad and painful backache. I decided to just hold her while I reclined on my bed for a minute to ease my back pain. She was on my hand that I rested on my pillow, next to my head. She stood there and watched me, but I was so tired and in so much pain, that I started to doze off. Sweetie Pea watched my eyelids, being so close to me and crawled off my hand and onto the pillow, right next to my head, across from my eyelids. She remained there and didn't wander off and then decided to take a snooze herself! Sweetie Pea stood there about a half hour, until I woke up.

How could a bug that is so small, assess a huge human being and understand that they have eyelids, when the Western conifer doesn't, and realize that the big human being was getting tired and had to sleep? And then decide to join in and take a nap right next to me?!! Extraordinary!

No one can comprehend, understand or accept, at this moment in time, the year 2020, that these bugs are far more intelligent, empathetic and sympathetic, than you can imagine!! They have reasoning intellect and act accordingly.

It's also amazing to watch them make decisions and here is an example. Sweetie Pea was out and crawling on my bed one time and looked over to see that I had different colored small fabrics on a tray that I used for the Western conifers' bed rolls. She picked out which one she liked the best, just by looking over at them and decided the burgundy-colored one was for her. She crawled over to it and up on it and remained there. I put the fabric into her container and she sat proudly on top of it. When I tried to get her to walk onto a green fabric piece, she wouldn't have any part of it. But she easily and eagerly crawled onto "her" burgundy fabric, whenever I lowered her while she was on my hand, into her container. She knew what she liked and she chose what she liked and wanted!

One day, she was in a very active crawling mode and she wouldn't sit still. She crawled all over my bedspread, my pant legs and my arms and hands for a very long time. Most of the time though, she liked to just sit with me, resting on my hand and or even watch TV with me! Then maybe she'd crawl a little bit.

The fact is, that these bugs have changing moods daily, just as we do. Sometimes we like to relax for a whole day and other times we want to be very active and the Western conifers are no different. Other times, Sweetie Pea was not satisfied to sit or be active and so we often refer to that as 'bitchy.' Aren't we all sometimes!!

Sweetie Pea was also tolerant of her babies, who crawled playfully onto her back and she looked over them with patience. They clung to her side and stayed close by and mimicked her when she drank. They stayed under or near her and they'd all watch each other. If the babies could see her, then they'd wander and crawl confidently all over the inside of the plastic container and on the screen. It kept Sweetie Pea amused and attentive to watch these small babies with all their energy, as she had a naturally calm disposition.

BUGS THAT LOVE! By Lori-Michele

Sweetie Pea and her baby.

Since the babies were so small, I removed the water dish at night, so as not to have any accidental drownings. Then in the morning, I'd put the cap back into their container with fresh sugar water. Sweetie Pea adapted to the routine and she'd be in the middle of her cage waiting for her breakfast, in the early morning hours. When I put the dish down, she'd readily get her breakfast and when she was full, she'd return up to perch on her favorite burgundy bed roll, to sit and relax.

BUGS THAT LOVE! By Lori-Michele

Butterscotch, who I named for her coloring, was found one day just outside the front door. Traumatized by a rough outdoor life, she had a missing back leg and a recently missing front left foot. I gently picked her up, but she squirmed and wriggled in my hand with immense fear and used these body movement tactics, hoping to scare me off. She must have done this often, as a defense mechanism, to ward off predators. She also flinched and ducked at the slightest sight of my fingers or hand, even if I was a foot away and I worried that she might be overreacting to shadows and have an eyesight problem. I had never had a conifer so fearful in all the years I've had them as pets.

Butterscotch kept holding her leg up, with the recently missing foot and every time she placed it down, she'd flinch in pain and pull it up again. I ever so gently, applied some Calmoseptine® on the end of the leg to coat it, so this would act like a bandage and hopefully block some of the pain when she tried to crawl. It worked and was like a little boot on the end of her leg.

I made sure my actions were slow, as to not frighten her. I held and talked to her gently each day and she slowly got more assurance and confidence, as she started to respond. After a couple of days, she didn't flinch as much and trusted me more. In just over a week, she became a very calm bug with a lovely temperament and now loved to be held for hours! This shows and proves how love and care can heal both physical and emotional injuries, for your pet Western conifers.

Butterscotch

BUGS THAT LOVE! By Lori-Michele

CHAPTER 7

HOW THEY PASS AWAY

Western Conifer Seed Bugs do not have a very long life expectancy. Some will only live a couple of months when you get them or up to a year. I have had so many adult conifers pass away and not in the same manner. Sometimes it'll be coming on just a day or two before or up to a week. Other times, they die suddenly, with no warning signs at all. Here are some examples: One died in the morning, while it was cleaning its antennae and I found it frozen in that position. One was simply walking along and died on the spot. Another one climbed up on the side of the screened cage and simply fell off backwards and died an hour later.

One conifer seemed totally normal and drank the day before, then went for a half hour walk the day of his death. When I put him back into his container, he seemed to be resting, but a couple hours later, he was dying. This happened again, with one who was all bright and alert and ready for the day in the morning. He went for a walk on the sofa chair and then slowed up and was dying in the afternoon.

One had a mishap and a back leg got torn off and it died the next day, from shock and trauma. (A note here: Many of the Western conifers will come in with a missing leg, but that doesn't hinder their life expectancy. They have even lost a leg while in their containers, but that has not hurt their longevity. Some rest a day or two after it happens, and yet others will be fine from that minute on and continue life, as if nothing ever happened! All of them never feel sorry for themselves if they lose a leg and they just adapt to the 'new' them and move on.)

So, sometimes, you can never tell how or when it's coming. Usually though, when it's time for them to pass, many try desperately to drink water for hours on end, especially a day or two before, but something inside them prevents this from happening and they tire from trying so hard. It's as if their body turns against them and shuts off the mechanism to suck up the water to drink, yet they try endlessly to do so until exhaustion, believing if they can just drink, they'll live, but instead, they die from dehydration. They slow down in energy and stop drinking and crawling. Their antennae start to go down and out to 180 degrees and they lose strength. You might notice that they haven't peed for a couple days and that their behavior has changed, losing their happy-go-lucky attitude.

When the death starts, there is nothing you can do to stop it. They have enough intelligence to sense when something is wrong with their bodies. The only thing you can do for them, is comfort them.

For some Western conifers, their antennae and/or their legs will twitch, shake or vibrate, as the hours pass and they get closer to death. I call this 'the shakes' and the males usually have this more than the females and die quicker. I believe it's their nervous system shutting down and these are the reactions. The males seem to suffer more, pulling legs in close to the body and contorting or writhing slowly, which I feel is indicative of pain, as they go through the dying process.

Also, some males develop a sickness, where they extend their appendage (see photo on page 60) and get a bit of a swollen abdomen and pass within one to three days.

Other Western conifers, both male and female, will simply lose strength and sit still, as they get weaker and their legs become limp and antennae will collapse flat, as they will drift away. I have often used a toothpick to gently straighten out the legs that have been drawn in and placed them in the position that the conifer always had when healthy, so it can feel 'normal,' at least psychologically. I feel that the conifers know that something bad is happening to them beyond their control and so by putting their legs back in a normal position because they can't do it themselves anymore, is reassuring for them.

Several have taken their last bit of strength to 'talk' to me and when I spoke their names to them, they have raised a foot or

BUGS THAT LOVE! By Lori-Michele

two in the palm of my hand and placed it back down, to tell me they were still there and could hear me and sometimes, I feel they were trying to ask me for help, to 'fix' them. They have also lifted either one or both antennae, when I have talked to them, as they are trying to communicate, with every ounce of energy they have left. It is heartbreaking, because I come to know their personalities and they become my pets and we develop a bond. They all know something is terribly wrong with them and they appreciate you holding and talking to them, while they pass.

Generally, it can take between several hours to days, for them to die. Typically, they pass within a day or two, but many go into a coma-like state, where they can't move or communicate, yet they are still alive. You can assess this by using a toothpick to gently hold up an antenna and then take the toothpick away. If the antenna goes down slowly, there is usually some life still left. If it drops immediately, you can assume that they have passed. And other times, if the antennae are completely stiff and have no flexibility, they are usually no longer there.

I have noticed many times, that when a Western conifer is picked on by another conifer repeatedly, they will die quicker. Bullying isn't good for humans or bugs and the ones that are picked on, are usually more sensitive and loving and they succumb to the stress. The males typically pick on each other more. It's a dominance thing, a bullying thing and unfortunately, a sexual thing. If there isn't a female around, the more aggressive male will try to mate with the weaker one, which only puts extreme stress on the conifer, as he can't defend or push off the stronger male. If he is continually picked on in this way, over and over again, he will usually be the first one to die.

But it can also happen with female bugs as well. *Sallie* was bullied by her roommate *Georgina*, who used to just crawl on and over her all the time. When Sallie had two accidents falling into the water, I blamed Georgina for pushing or knocking her in because of her aggressive and bullying nature.

One day Sallie didn't look right, as her antennae seemed too flat.

BUGS THAT LOVE! By Lori-Michele

I tried to lift her up and although she was weak, she knew what I was trying to do, so she reached her right foot forward and up, to climb aboard my finger. With all her might, she lifted her own body up, giving more strength than she had, to assist me in lifting her up, so she could be with me. I raised her up and out of her container and put her in my hand, where she then rested, but continued to pass. So sweet and loving, she still responded when I talked to or touched her, and she moved her antennae now and again. She raised her wings up and out, before she let them fall into place again and I've only seen a few conifers exhibit this behavior near death.

With both males and females who are bullied, you don't assume it's occurring often because you can't watch them every minute. I do believe it's the heightened level of stress hormones that bring on an early death to them. So, if you see it happening, try to separate the gentle ones from the aggressive ones.

Another story I'd like to share is about a conifer named *Prancer*, who reached out to communicate to me, even though I thought he had passed away nine hours before because his body was completely loose- a sign that they are no longer here.

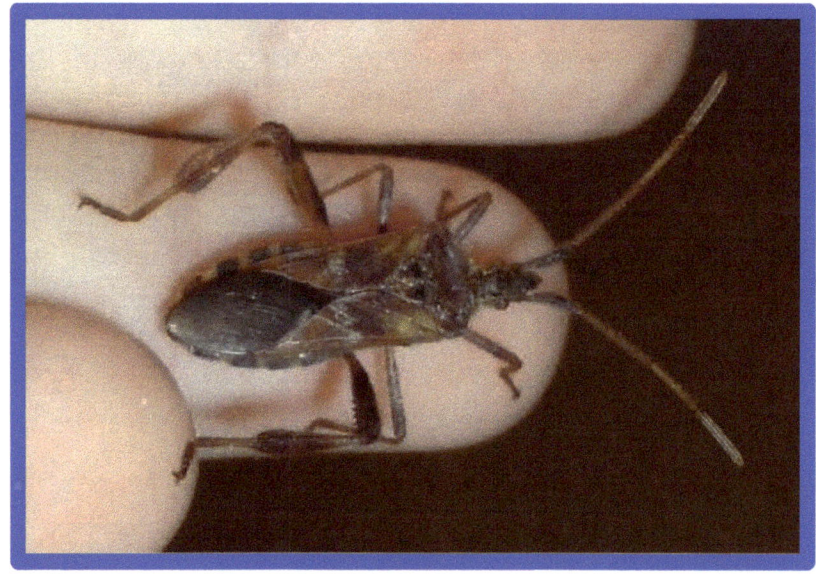

Prancer

BUGS THAT LOVE! By Lori-Michele

I kept him near me on the right arm of the sofa chair and as I held another male bug that night, I said similar sayings to that bug, that I had also spoken to Prancer. I glanced over to him and was shocked to see that Prancer had lifted his left antenna up! He had heard my voice and remembered those sayings and he was responding to me. The poor thing thought I was speaking those familiar sayings to him! It was so touching and broke my heart and yet it was also startling! I thought he had already passed, but I picked him up again right away, when I saw that he lifted his antenna and I spoke to him for an hour, giving him all my attention and love.

Another thing is because these conifers spend a long time together, several months, as a small or large group, they actually bond together and become like sisters or brothers. They adapt to each other's personalities and some become the best of friends. When one starts to die, a healthy conifer will walk over to and examine the dying one's entire body with their labium, even crawling on top of it to do so. For ones that don't care or have a tough attitude, they will simply walk off the dying one and go on with their life.

I had two female conifers, *Magic* and *Big Girl*, that had lived together for a number of months and when Magic was dying, Big Girl inspected her with her labium and then stood by her. She left briefly to get a drink and returned to the toilet paper bed they shared and rested her feet gently on Magic's body and legs. She stood next to her, touching the dying one, keeping her feet on her in a loving way, throughout the entire night and stood awake, to comfort her dying sister. Somehow she knew that Magic was very sick and dying and she wouldn't leave her side for a minute or go to sleep. (If the Western conifers antennae are up, they are not sleeping.)

Big Girl stood with her until the end, as Magic died slowly throughout the night. In the morning, she wouldn't leave her sister's side and I had to gently encourage her to crawl onto my finger to move her away from the deceased one. Big Girl was completely exhausted from staying up all night and I put her into a little bed roll of her own, where she instantly went to sleep from pure exhaustion. This goes to show how much these bugs care, love and have compassion for each other.

Big Girl (left) comforting Magic (right).

When Western Conifer Seed Bugs have passed, sometimes they have an odor of pistachio nuts and old, dried and decaying leaves. They do not change much in appearance after death, some get a little darker in color, but you can keep them in a little box if you wish. They become a little lighter in weight, but they do not physically change at all or decay, if kept in climate-controlled area.

I have wondered if they died from some genetic disease or just old age, but it still puzzles me why they seem healthy one day and dying the next because there isn't much warning.

BUGS THAT LOVE! By Lori-Michele

I do believe that 'love' makes them last longer than they would, if they lived the rest of their lives outside. They know that you care for and love them by talking to and holding them. They can sense who is a good person and who isn't.

So, although genetics; an outdoor-caught disease; poor nutrition; stress; bad weather and elements, might have shortened their lives before you came to rescue them and provide nutritious sugar water, a soft bed and safety, at least now they will have comfort and love from you, until they do pass on. And that makes all the difference in the world to them!

BUGS THAT LOVE! By Lori-Michele

CHAPTER 8

MORE STUDY NEEDED AND WHAT CAN BE LEARNED FROM THEM

So much more study needs to be done on the Western Conifer Seed Bug. I believe that they, as well as some other special bugs, that have not been studied enough, have some important hidden answers to our own diseases.

I'm convinced because of what happened to *Buggy* and how he recovered from his stroke-like symptoms, that there is a hidden secret answer there, for us humans to benefit from, by studying how they are capable of recovering from it.

Our world is full of answers to all of the physical problems, aliments and diseases that we humans have, but not many people want to think outside the box and lead the way, to all the discoveries awaiting and that are right in front of us, in nature.

Bugs and their natural immunological systems have some of the answers and they need to be studied and revealed for our benefit. There might be a correlation between these particular bugs and humans that would be worth the study and research.

Most entomologists are unsympathetic and/or unknowledgeable about the Western Conifer Seed Bug, as they are taught incorrectly. They have no idea that these bugs have feelings, memories, decision-making and learning abilities, plus the cleverness of finding ways to communicate with you. Entomologists completely dismiss the notion of the Western conifer's ability to love and their intelligence because they are not shown to look for these things or that they matter.

When I asked several entomologists for help concerning a cracked labium on a conifer, many were unconcerned with giving me advice for what to do and simply didn't care. I'm sorry to say, but most of these professionals will study only briefly what others have told them about these little creatures and leave it at

BUGS THAT LOVE! By Lori-Michele

that. They mainly study ways to kill them, and they do not learn about the conifer's intelligence, behavior, emotions, or anything else! I was told with derogatory expression, "Well, as far as the intelligence of bugs goes...." and "If a bug tries to escape, is it because they have emotions?.... I don't think so!" and "We're trying to find ways to kill them, not save them!"

This is completely and entirely the wrong way to think about or approach these small, loving, sensitive and intelligent creatures. Western conifers and many other bugs, have much to teach us and we have so much to learn from them! They hold the secrets to our own survival, which have not been studied, in a positive way at all.

I can only hope that the entomologists change their way of thinking, in the future. It all starts with caring and sharing and showing others to look more closely at the wonder of what is right in front of us and totally ignored. The answers lie in what is not studied, dismissed and overlooked.

BUGS THAT LOVE! By Lori-Michele

CHAPTER 9

SPECIAL SECTION ON SHIELD BUGS AND SOME SIMILARITIES WITH WESTERN CONIFER SEED BUGS

The disdain for Shield Bugs, also referred to as "stink bugs," comes from misinformation, to scare people into instantly disliking them, from that given name. It has been reported that they omit an odor when they are killed, hence the name "stink bug" which heightens the animosity for them. The fact is, that almost any bug that is smashed, would omit an odor of some kind.

It is also falsely reported that if they are frightened, they omit and spray this odor on someone, but it simply isn't true. This myth needs to be dispelled. I have had many dozens of these bugs as pets and in the initial stages of trying to catch them quickly and not knowing me, they surely would have been frightened in some way, yet they never sprayed anything on me, not even once!

These are misunderstood creatures, that can seem at first, cold and unfriendly because of their appearance, with an armor-type shield for their back, but I can assure you that they are warm and friendly, highly intelligent and loving. They learn and adapt readily. These bugs love encouragement and understand when I'm reassuring or consoling them.

<u>Both Shield Bugs and Western Conifer Seed Bugs are fast movers, when you find them</u>. It takes love and patience for them to come around and conform to your ways, but they are smart, loving and do so willingly.

<u>Shield bugs get along with Western conifers wonderfully</u>, sharing the water dish and even a bed roll or a screen together. They will not crawl on or bully a conifer at all. They will touch with their antennae, to check each other out, but they will keep their distance and act politely, as they share their quarters with the conifers. I witnessed one conifer walk up to and touch the back of a Shield bug and then sleep comfortably, right next to him.

BUGS THAT LOVE! By Lori-Michele

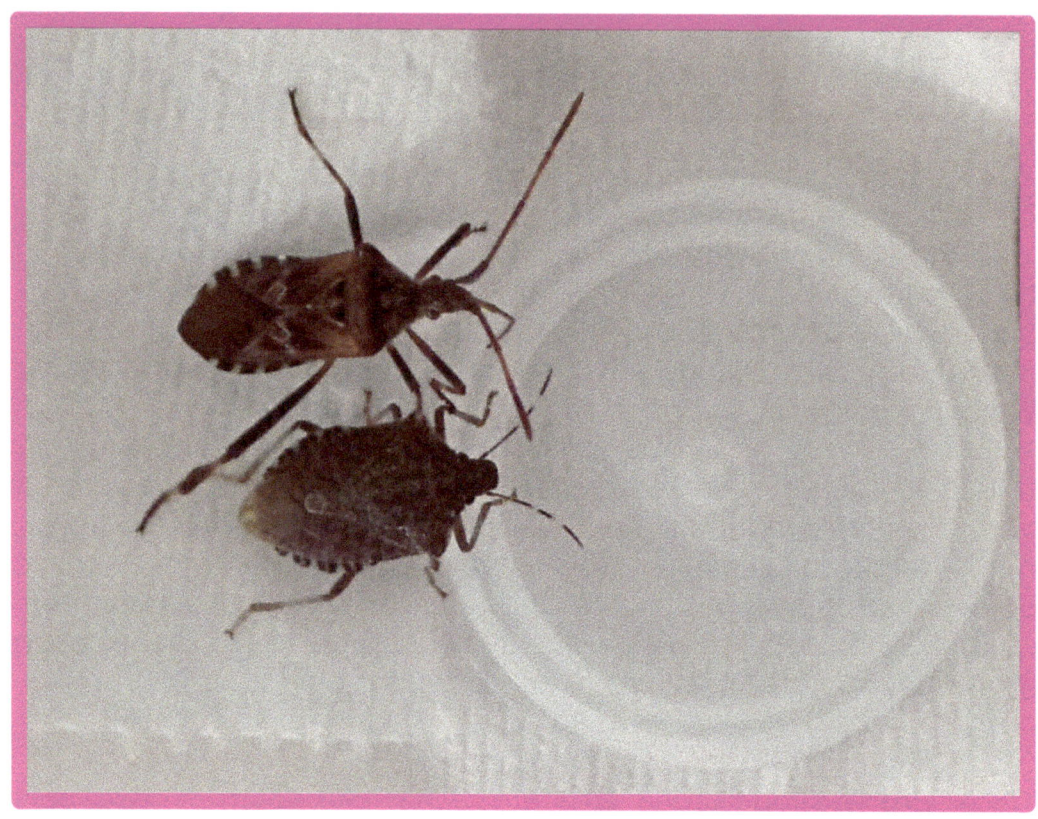

Ballerina, the Western Conifer Seed Bug and Betsy, the Shield Bug, who were the best of friends.

<u>Both Shield bugs and Western conifers have adaptability and can be reprogrammed.</u> One example is that in the wild, Shield bugs associate any form of touch on their back or 'shield' as a threat. Conifers do the same with anything that touches their back legs. After talking quietly and stroking them gently on these areas, they now come to associate touch as caring and security and they don't see it as a threat anymore.

<u>Both Shield bugs and Western conifers have memories.</u>
Wendy, a Shield bug, and *Cookie*, a Western conifer, had frozen most of the night, since the temperature dropped and I didn't have the heat on.

I had forgotten to put them into their bed roll the night before, so there wasn't anything to hide in or under, in their container. When I got up in the morning and saw my mistake, I held both of them in my hands, to warm them up.

I heated up their bed roll in front of the space heater, as they watched and when they saw me lower and place it before them in my hand, they both eagerly started crawling towards and then into it because they had remembered it was a place of great warmth. They didn't care that it was now morning time, they just headed there quickly to get and stay warm!!

As I mentioned earlier, both types of bugs have memories, such as: remembering where their water dish and homes are; how to play games; returning to you after flights; friends and foes of their own kind or another; and of course, facial recognition of you!

<u>Both species of bugs know each other's body language and can sense when one another is distressed.</u> Wendy, a Shield bug, wanted to crawl a lot, despite being so crippled with only two legs that actually worked and two that were not fully functional. (She had previously lost two legs before she came into the house a year before.) I watched, as both her and Cookie, a conifer, were crawling on my bed.

Wendy seemed particularly stressed, as she was desperately trying to pull herself forward to crawl on the blanket, but to no avail. She was rapidly moving her antennae around and feeling the blanket in front of her.

Cookie watched her behavior and then walked over and placed her front right foot on Wendy's left backside and Wendy immediately calmed down, stopped moving her antennae and felt reassured that it was ok, just as if I had touched her back and talked to her to calm down. Cookie sensed and knew that Wendy was upset and sought out to help her; then gave her comfort by telling her it was okay in her own way. I had never seen one type of bug relate to the other in this way before and then walk over to reassure her.

BUGS THAT LOVE! By Lori-Michele

These bugs have more empathy and understanding than we can imagine and then they even act on it, to help one another! Both of these female bugs became very dependent on each other for company and even rested next to each other and touched feet. I believe it gave both of them comfort, that someone else was there for a companion.

About Shield Bugs only.
Sometimes when the Shield bug is new to you and your home, they are hyper, fearful, anxious and don't trust anyone or anything. Most adapt and overcome all of this very quickly, when you feed them daily and they realize that you are there to help and protect them and not hurt them.

It's easy enough to pick them up, since their body size is usually a ½ to 5/8ths of an inch long. Just imagine if you were to pick up an M & M's® candy, since they are similar in size and shape. They will crawl quickly onto your fingers.

Most of the time, Shield bugs know that you are not to be "tapped" like a maple tree, when you hold them. You'll notice that sometimes they'll 'lick' you, as they crawl around and examine your hand and arm. They actually know it's you by doing this and that you are not something to eat. You can see and feel, a bit of dispersed clear liquid from their labium (drinking straw), as they drag it beneath them and onto your hand, fingers or arm. It's harmless and they are only 'testing' and identifying you, the same way a dog would use his nose.

They like to hide in and under the toilet paper or Kleenex® that you line on the bottom of their holding containers, as well as their cloth bed rolls. When replacing the liners, be sure to check them thoroughly because these bugs are rather flat and can be easily overlooked and thrown out, if they are hiding or sleeping.

A special bond.
One Shield bug knew the touch and warmth of my hand, like a newborn baby knows its mother. When I put her into my father's hand, she squirmed and panicked and kept crawling around

BUGS THAT LOVE! By Lori-Michele

restlessly in his palm. When I took her back, she settled immediately into my hand and wasn't upset anymore. It could be that she knew my body temperature and certain pulsating blood beat, as I held and talked to her often. I feel that these bugs bond with you. They adapt to your vocal sounds and 'attach' themselves to you, knowing that you are there to care for them and keep them safe. And some pick you out as their favorite!

<u>These bugs are trainable and follow routine.</u>
They know breakfast time, playtime and bedtime! Every morning, I would get a cap of fresh sugar water and I'd lift off the top of the screening and call down to the Shield bugs, in their container, "Breakfast!" and *Window* especially would look up at me and wave his antennae around all excited. Then I'd place the water down and he'd come running towards the cap, crawl a bit up the side and happily start drinking. How he loved breakfast!

<u>Playtime & games.</u>
For playtime, *Buttercup* liked to crawl up my hand and then fly to my other hand, that I held out a distance away and then we'd repeat this game over and over. When tired, she'd just rest on my thumb.

I've had several Shield bugs that liked to play this repetitious game, as well as 'fly to the drape' where I'd hold two Shield bugs, one on each hand, and stand about eight feet from the window drapes. Then I'd ask them, "Are you ready to fly?!!" and excitedly they flap their wings a bit and I'd continue, "Well, okay... fly to the drape!!" and they'd take off and fly straight there. Then I'd collect them off the drapes and they'd sit still on my fingers while I carried them back to where we started and I'd repeat what I said and they'd do it all over again. Many would do this for such a long while, that I'd get tired before they would, playing this game!

When playtime is over and I lower my hand, while holding a Shield bug or a Western conifer into their containers, they act a bit differently. Most conifers will freeze and refuse to crawl off

BUGS THAT LOVE! By Lori-Michele

because they don't want playtime to end. The ones that do so willing, are either tired or thirsty or look forward to being back in their safe and cozy home.

With Shield bugs, they learn the routine quickly and understand that after playtime, I will be putting them back in their container and as I lower my hand near their safe home, they will often just jump/fly right into the container, without a problem at all!

<u>Bedtime.</u>
Shield bugs know when I'm putting them to bed, as they will freeze and look straight ahead when I put the bed roll close to their feet, but they will move their antennae, as I talk encouragingly to them. They will then step forward and crawl into the bed, as I continue to talk to them and tell them it's bedtime. I truly believe they understand. If they didn't, they would stay in one place and refuse to budge. They have a strong disposition and I believe they know I'm caring for them and have their best interest in mind.

Some will crawl into the bed roll quickly, if they are especially tired, because they know this is a place of security and comfort and it is now the time for rest and sleep. When they have crawled into the bed roll, I then place it down into their containers.

<u>The nice part about these bugs is that they can eat a variety of foods and they live longer.</u> These bugs have their own preferences for different foods. They all love sugar water, but most like watermelon, apples and canned peas. They can also eat raw green bell peppers, plums, nectarines, peaches and apricots. But I found out that no one liked zucchini or eggplant. Some prefer to pierce through the skins to eat, but if you just slice fruits or vegetables, it's easier for them and most prefer it that way. Organic fruits and vegetables are your best bet.

BUGS THAT LOVE! By Lori-Michele

One Shield bug eating on top of a slice of watermelon.

Several Shield bugs enjoying cut-up pieces of watermelon.

BUGS THAT LOVE! By Lori-Michele

A Shield bug enjoying a squished pea.

A Shield bug eating a piece of green bell pepper.

BUGS THAT LOVE! By Lori-Michele

Five Shield bugs drinking together.

Shield bugs show and express body language.
When a Shield bug does not want to go where you want to put them, they tell you so, through body language. As you carry them on your finger or hand and attempt to 'let them off' on a piece of cloth, clothing, material, or furniture, they will instantly stop and not move. They communicate that this is not where they want to go or be 'dropped off' and when you pull your hand away, they start moving their antennae happily again and are satisfied that they can stay just where they are.

Also, if you touch the side of a Shield bug while drinking, most will 'wave' their butt back and forth as if to say "Go away, I'm drinking, don't bother me!"

One particular Shield bug loved when I talked to her and would raise her head up to look at me, while she waved her antennae joyfully. As I continued to speak to her, she wanted to talk back to me, so she'd move her left front foot forward and back several times. It was her gesture of saying to me, "I'm excited to hear and see you and I have much to say as well!"

Wanting to be with you.
It amazes me how these bugs think and react. I kept a couple female Shield bugs in one container together. One of them slept all the time. The other one ran around in the container, especially near the top and it just wanted to be let out.

When I opened the screen, she walked onto the other screen tops nearby and didn't fly off. I thought she had stored-up energy, but she just wanted human touch and to be held! I put my finger out for her to crawl on and then she sat there cheerfully, as I talked to her and was now quite content.

Common sense & safety.
One day when *Buttercup* was flying about, she got lost and scared behind a mini-blind, so she sought out shelter to wait for me to find her. She hid under the rubber stopper that held the window open, as it had a piece cut out in the center and so to her, it was like a cave. When frightened, lost or confused, these bugs seek safety and shelter.

Consideration of others.
Window, couldn't really walk around very much anymore, due to advanced age. I'd put him on the arm of the sofa chair and then I put the newer, younger bug *Wendall* next to him.

Wendall would venture off and crawl up the arm of the chair and across the top, but he would then turn around and come back to the spot where Window was. He'd then sit next to Window to

BUGS THAT LOVE! By Lori-Michele

keep him company, but would leave for a short time to get a drink from the sugar water cap, that I placed on the arm chair. He also crawled onto the pine piece I placed there and hung around, looking over at Window.

Wendall seemed to know and understand that Window was old and slower and adapted his behavior. He accepted that just hanging out on the sofa chair together was now the 'new normal.'

Overcoming a problem.
I did have one Shield bug that was resistant to drinking at first. It simply would not adapt to drinking over the low-edged bottle cap.

I decided to give it droplets of the sugar water on the floor of the plastic container, I kept it in. Then I tried to give it droplets on the screening and it drank that way for a while. Then I placed him directly on an apple slice, but it still took time for him to taste it.

Because this Shield bug had a couple of missing legs on its right side, balancing was difficult and its fear was falling into the water cap.

Although another Shield bug had the exact same thing, it didn't have any fear and learned on his own how to maneuver his body the right way to get a drink. But this one just wouldn't overcome its fear no matter what.

I decided to place him on a piece of a flat pine bush clipping, that I put a bit on and over the water dish. He then inched his way ever so slowly, feeling with his antennae, up the pine piece and closer to the water dish. He now felt safe and secure with his footing on the pine piece, as he slowly pulled his drinking straw forward and lowered it down into the water cap and drank away!

Only once, when he was really thirsty, did he overcome his fear and marched straight up to the cap to get a drink, with no problem, but then he reverted to being scared again later.

<u>Shield bugs are also known to respond to human medication.</u>
A few of the Shield bugs have developed 'bumble foot.' This is when a strange thickening appears that looks like gray material, such as a piece of lint that seems to be tightly wound around their antenna or foot. It is a mistake to try and remove it yourself, like I did.

Even though I very delicately tried to remove it with a thin sewing needle and even used a magnifying glass to help me along, so I wouldn't injure the antenna or foot, (and afterwards, the bugs felt it to be so freeing because the thickness of the 'material' that weighed them down, was now removed), it didn't solve the problem and they died shortly afterwards- a few days to a week.

It seems that this strange gray thing that suddenly appears and gets thicker either on a foot or antenna, is a fungus of some sort. So when it happened to a third Shield bug, I decided to apply an over-the-counter human medication that treats fungus, called Calmoseptine®.

I used a Q-tip® and gently applied it over the gray bundle on the foot and leg of one that had this affliction. After a couple days, I applied more. (Whenever you see the pinkness of the product disappearing, apply more, even though the Shield bug will be dragging the weight of the fungus and the weight of the creamy medication.)

To my surprise, after a few more days of application, the 'bumble foot' was totally gone and he had his normal foot back! On top of that, it never came back! It also worked on the antenna of another Shield bug.

It is surprising and pleasing to know that a human medication can cure a bug of their illness!

BUGS THAT LOVE! By Lori-Michele

<u>Trying an experiment.</u>
With *Tempi*, the two-spotted Shield bug, he had a little body clock that got up at the same time each morning and boy did he look forward to breakfast! He easily adapted and learned how to drink from the sugar-water filled cap and climbed up quickly to drink. He was small, but very loving and enjoyed being held. Often, he would take a snooze right on my finger!

When he got older- 8 months- he seemed to slow down and the bright reddish markings amongst the black on his back, started to lighten up to a light orange coloring.

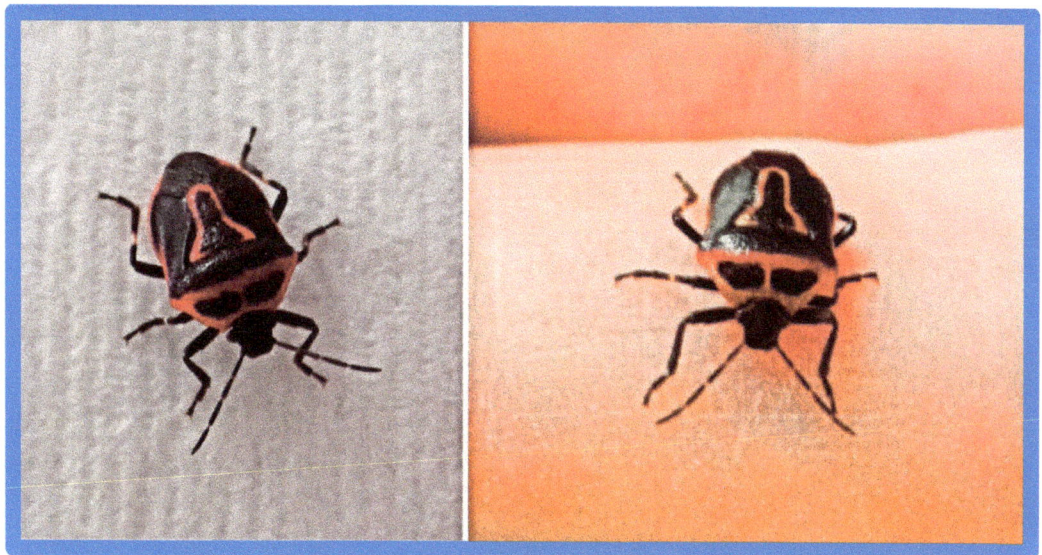

Tempi with red markings; later, lighter orange when sick.

Tempi was starting to slow down with his play time and suddenly he didn't want to drink anymore, so I knew he was sick. Desperate to try to extend his life, I experimented by giving him a small trace amount of a mild antibiotic in his drinking water, just two times. This seemed to help him, as he got a little more energy and started drinking again. Tempi lasted another week before he passed away and I wondered if it was from a virus, bacteria or disease of some kind, as I just don't believe it was old age.

BUGS THAT LOVE! By Lori-Michele

I also tried this with a Western conifer named Johnny. He too, became ill and was dying, so with nothing to lose, I put a small amount of antibiotic in his drinking sugar water and it helped him live a few more days, before he passed as well.

Although I don't recommend experimenting with antibiotics for your pet bugs, I tried it because I wanted to find a way to cure what was making them ill. Since it gave them a few extra days to a week to live, it did help a small bit, but ultimately they still died. My hope is that someday in the future, people might care enough to study the use of medicines on special bugs, such as the ones I'm discussing in this book, to cure illness and extend their lives and that they will be loved and cared for as much as other pets, like cats and dogs.

Shield bug babies.
Sometimes, a female Shield bug pet might lay some eggs, either on the bed roll or most likely, the screening on top of its container. They will be in a cluster of many and are extremely light green in color, almost whitish and round-shaped.

When they hatch, the little ones need to be left alone for up to three days and they do not need anything to drink, until they do their first molt. Just like conifers, they leave their papery black skin behind, but are white and pinkish-red initially, before darkening as the hours pass.

After their first molting, you can try to give them something to drink by pouring some watered-down sugar water onto some toilet paper and have the babies crawl onto it. Or you can dip a Q-tip® into some sugar water and have them crawl onto the end and drink from there.

The babies should be played with twice a day, in order to work up an appetite and continue to grow and stay alive. They have a tendency to gather together in a group and just stay put, which will only make them get weaker, as they won't feel the need to get a drink and grow. They will be very active for a short amount of time and it's healthy for them to get this exercise.

BUGS THAT LOVE! By Lori-Michele

Shield bug eggs, hatching (center) & after the first molt.

About a couple weeks after they hatch, you can try giving them some bean sprouts to stab into and drink. Squeeze the bean sprouts first to soften them up and it'll be easier for the baby Shield bugs to taste the liquid from them and drink it. This helps with their nutrition.

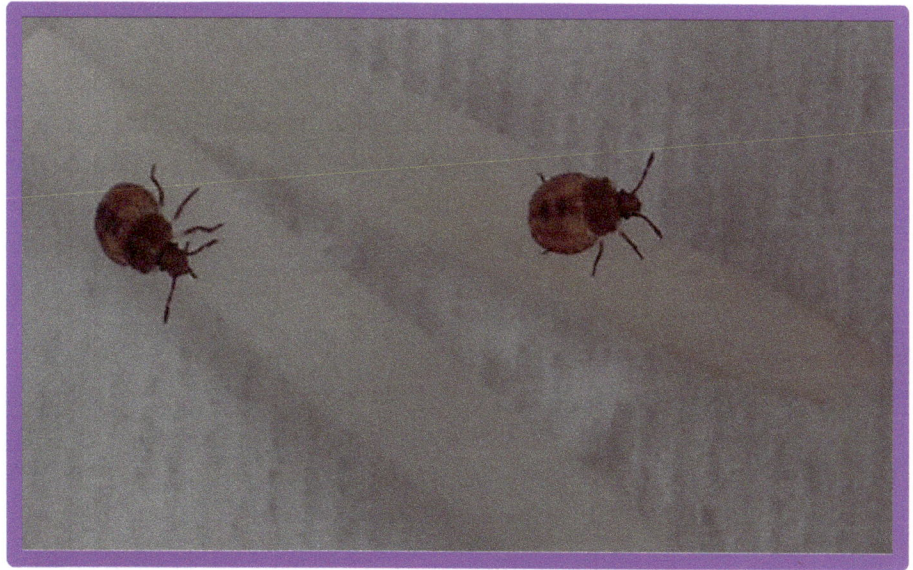

Two baby Shield bugs drinking the juice from bean sprouts.

Shield bugs go through 5 molts and it's rare for the babies to reach adulthood, but one or two might surprise you!

BUGS THAT LOVE! By Lori-Michele

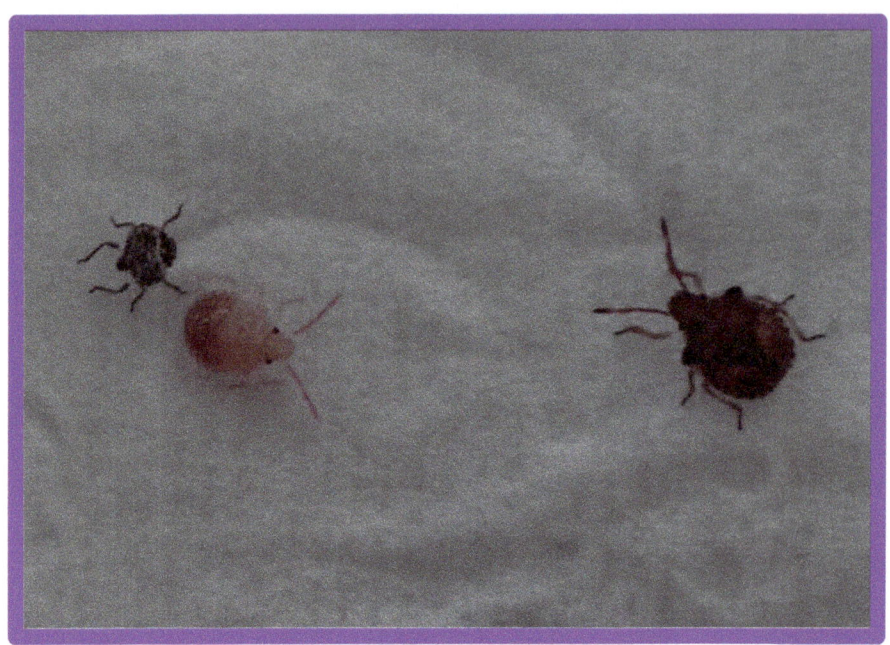

Two Shield bugs after their 3rd molt. Notice the old skin left behind on the left. Also, see how the bug darkens in color, who molted earlier, on the right.

Something surprising about genetics.
Sometimes you might get a bug that is just odd and you can't figure out why. I had a female Shield bug pet, that I named *Spunky*. She was odd in a strange way, that she kept stabbing the inside of the plastic container she was kept in with her drinking straw, as if she was sticking it into an apple piece or some kind of vegetable.

She'd stab the plastic deeply and just remain that way for hours, thinking she'd eventually get liquid of some kind. She did this all the time, even when she already drank from the water cap and didn't have a need for thirst. I tried to give her different things to eat or dig into, but she always returned to stabbing the plastic.

Well, she was friends with her roommate *Petunia*, and they walked everywhere together and cleaned their antennae at the same time and even drank from the water cap together…. until Petunia slowed down, became sick and started to die.

BUGS THAT LOVE! By Lori-Michele

Petunia & Spunky when friends, drinking together.

In the morning, I found Spunky with her front legs on Petunia's back, as she was literally stabbing her labium right into and sucking the fluid out of Petunia's body!

I was appalled at the sight of what was occurring and it took forever to get Spunky to withdraw her drinking straw from Petunia's back, plus it left a puncture mark! Needless to say, Petunia died shortly afterward.

But this made me wonder... can Shield bugs tell when the other is sick and dying? Do they then think this is a meal to survive on? Or was Spunky just one demented and twisted bug, out of a species that normally has good behavior and wouldn't act in this barbaric way?!!

Just a week later, Spunky laid eggs and I now wondered, was she trying to get nutrients to feed her eggs, even if that meant being cannibalistic?

BUGS THAT LOVE! By Lori-Michele

Sadly, she was now in the container by herself and she acted differently. It appeared that she had remorse for what she did and was sad about it. She never regained her 'spunk' for which I named her. I found that I couldn't hold or love her the way I did before and she acted differently when I held her, never being her happy true self again.

When her two babies hatched, she didn't take much interest in them and she just sat quietly in her container and would get a drink daily, but didn't do much else. The babies stood near her, but she wasn't interested in them. Two weeks after they hatched, she died. A sad end for all. But, it didn't end there… genetics are passed on and repeated behaviors come out of it.

Spunky and her two babies.

BUGS THAT LOVE! By Lori-Michele

The only one of Spunky's babies to survive was *Pillow*. This bug followed the same pattern as its mother. Pillow was best friends with a Western conifer named *Mini* and followed her around like the conifer was a mother figure, even hiding next to or underneath her. Then when Mini got sick and weak, I found Pillow with his drinking straw deeply embedded into Mini's back, drawing up her fluids!

Again, I was appalled and I feel that this made Mini die quicker. Whatever Mini had to cause her death, caused Pillow's death by doing what he did and he died a few weeks later. Diseases seem to be transmissible between the two bugs.

So the question is: Why did the Shield bugs do this and turn on their friends when they knew they were weak and sick and close to death? The whole thing sickens me, but it might prove that genetics come into play here. The old adage, 'the apple doesn't fall far from the tree,' proved true in this case. Spunky did it and then her offspring Pillow did it! I doubt any study has been done about this genetic pattern behavior, but there you have it.

<u>Their own secrets.</u>
I have noticed that these Shield bugs, without seeing each other, will suddenly stop and start to clean their antennae and legs, as if there is a certain pull from the universe that only they can feel, like an internal body clock. This happened one day Sept. 1, 2017 at 3:25 pm. I had three of them crawling on me at once and they were in different areas where one couldn't see the other, yet they all stopped and started to clean their antennae at the same time!

They also talk to each other through buzzing of their bodies, that you and I can't hear. As two female Shield bugs were walking on my hand, the dominant one was walking and touching the other and I could feel the vibration. I believe that the buzzing one, was talking to the other.

<u>Just so you know.</u>
When Shield bugs start to pass away, I make sure to touch and

BUGS THAT LOVE! By Lori-Michele

talk to them a lot. They will move their feet and legs out a little bit and move their antennae, to respond to you and to 'tell' you that they are there, until they are no longer able to do so. It is very touching. They appreciate the reassurance and love you give to them during this terrible time.

The mysterious paralyzation occurs with both Shield bugs and Western conifers, when death comes. They don't want to die and they try non-stop to fight against it and live, but the turn-off process takes over, preventing them from drinking and they ultimately pass slowly from dehydration.

Mysteries of Shield bugs.
Shield bugs do some things that are still a mystery to me. A lot of the time, when at least two of them are in the same container, they will touch faces and stay that way for quite a while. Also, when a lot of Shield bugs are in one container, sometimes they will line up in a row. I still don't know why they do this or what it means, but I'd sure like to know!

Two Shield bugs touching faces together.

BUGS THAT LOVE! By Lori-Michele

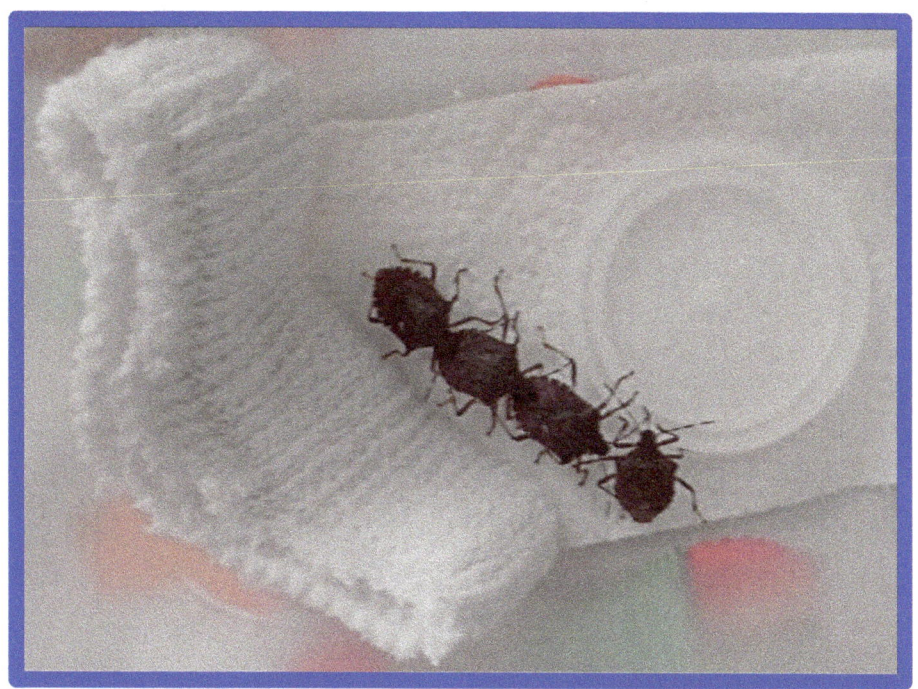

A row of male Shield bugs, but why do they do this?

Here is one story about a pet Shield bug I had, named Gusto.

Gusto's story:

When I first found *Gusto*, he was on the inside of the storm window in April 2013 and was desperately using his drinking straw to find liquid off the totally dry window. I opened the main window, reached my hand up and gently grabbed him, as he fell into my hand. I brought him in and gave him sugar water on the floor and he drank for three hours!

After that, he was determined to continue walking everywhere with such gusto, that's what I named him. He would randomly just take off in flight to a window or the ceiling lamp.

Initially, he was extremely independent and determined to do as he wanted, but totally fearful of the 'fingers.' He saw me as a threat and would not crawl onto my fingers, but avoid them at all costs. He'd lower his antennae and turn away. So I started guiding him where I wanted him to go by holding my hand above and near him and he'd turn, walking quickly, in whichever direction I wanted him to go.

After a month or so, he realized that those 'fingers' were not there to hurt him, but help him and I 'rescued' him several times when he got into predicaments. He'd wander too far, go up too high on a wall or drape, just freeze in place on an individual mini-blind, crawl around till exhaustion or just find himself lost and then suddenly... the 'fingers' would appear and he was thankful! He'd now reach out and crawl rapidly onto them and hold on steady, as I lowered him from his high or unusual place, to safety. He then began enjoying rides on my finger, as I walked back and forth across the room and he loved the wind and speed, while he hung on.

Gusto found a place to sleep in a crook of a paper J.C. Penney® bag, that was in the living room. It had a fold in it and was like a little cave. So, after he played all day, I'd let him crawl off my hand and onto that bag and he'd walk into that crevice, turn around, back up into it and look out at me and the world. He'd then sleep there all night. Soon enough though, he found a better place.

I don't know how it happened or when, but one day when I looked all over for him because he was missing, I found him in the big paperback cookbook, on the end table, between the cover and first page. He felt at home there and very safe and made it his new sleeping area.

He developed a complete routine and never ventured far. He would get up at 2 p.m. and crawl within the perimeters of the end table, never venturing beyond there. He crawled back and forth across the end table, but would not go down the legs or edge of it. He crawled in and out of the two books on the table; onto the remote control, the lamp wire, and his favorite place was the stand-up picture frame- where he'd crawl up to the top and across, down the front and sides of it and then even hide

BUGS THAT LOVE! By Lori-Michele

under the frame stem in the back.

Sometimes, when he was loaded with energy and felt like flying, I'd turn on the ceiling lamp. He'd fly circularly around the lamp, making big and smaller-sized concentric circles, having such a glorious fun time, around and around- 60 or more times, (and once over 150!) and then even change direction mid-way and go the opposite way! When he got tired, he'd dash to the left and right and then suddenly land perfectly in a dead stop, on the back of my hand or arm, my upper back and a few times right on the top of my head! I'd grab him gently and place him near his water dish, where he'd readily drink and then climb into his bed, in the book, as he knew playtime and exercise were over. Then he'd wash up, cleaning his front and second feet and sometimes third pair, as well as his antennae.

I noticed that he liked to rest at the end of the day, on the soft drape. So, I got a piece of soft white cloth and put it into the smaller, exercise book. He had been switching books to sleep in whenever he wanted- sometimes it was the cookbook and other times, the exercise book. He'd just crawl up and into them. A couple times, when he wanted to be cozy, he'd climb into the second or third page of the cookbook, as to have a more confined shelter overhead, since the pages were closer together.

One night, I took tired little Gusto off the drape and let him crawl off my finger, as he stepped onto the cloth. At first, he was unsure of it and slept on the white page of the book, right next to the cloth. But the next night he crawled onto it. He then loved to crawl all around on it and turn around to face out, to see me and wash up. He'd listen with his antennae up or half down as I watched TV. When it was time to turn out the lights, I tell him "Night-night Gusto, it's time to go to bed." In the morning, I'd find that he had backed up further into the book and/or gotten into a comfy fold of the cloth, with his antennae flat down. He was asleep completely.

Gusto adapted to a sugar water dish and when he was thirsty, he knew just where to go to get a drink. He enjoyed a slice of

BUGS THAT LOVE! By Lori-Michele

watermelon and he ate plums and nectarines, but peaches were his favorite.

Another time, I discovered that he loved to play a little game. While sitting down, I'd let him crawl down the length of my thigh to my knee, as I would say to him, "run, run, run," since he was so full of energy! Then when he got to the edge of my knee he'd stop, look down and over, then turn around and race back towards me, as I'd clap my hands in front of him and yell, "Yaaay, yaaay, Gusto!" He'd race-walk towards me faster, as I shouted all excitedly and then I'd place my open palm down, fingers together, on my upper thigh and he'd crawl right onto them. I'd raise my hand up and praise him and then I'd place him down and we'd do the whole routine all over again. We must have done this over 20 times and it was just so much fun for the both of us!

I think the more time, love and attention you give a bug, the more you get back. You can probably train them to do tricks, if enough time was spent with them. And they do respond to encouragement!

One time Gusto fell backwards into his sugar water and this made his wings stick together on his back, when it dried. I helped get them unstuck by pouring water onto his back, while he used his back legs to try and get them loose, and I blew air on his back, until the wings finally undid. We had worked quite a while at this and Gusto knew what I was trying to do. When he got them unstuck, I continued to blow air on his back and he fanned and flapped them several times to make sure they were in good working order. He seemed to have trusted me more after his stuck-wings incident. Whenever I blew air on him, after that, he seemed to think that it was 'motherly' of me.

Gusto also gave me signals to communicate with me. When he didn't want to get off my finger because he wanted to continue to play, he'd simply freeze in place or back up and turn around quickly.

BUGS THAT LOVE! By Lori-Michele

When I tried to wake him up or if he didn't want to move from his spot, he wiggled his bottom back and forth, as if to say "No, I'm not moving from here, go away!" and not to bother him!

One time he got lost for almost a day and when I found him, he signaled to me that he was thirsty by holding his drinking straw out. I got him some sugar water and he drank for over an hour.

Another time, when I put him on the edge of the book, I said, "You can go to bed now. Go to bed now," and he listened! He crawled forward and made a left, going deeper towards the spine of the book. Then he turned around and started to clean his antennae.

Gusto loved to bask in the sun near the window. He also loved to crawl on my shirt, up to my soft collar and was perfectly content to sit there and look out at everything, as I walked around or sat down. He also liked to watch all the action and activity of people in the house, from the top of the drape, looking down. Sometimes he would just want to sit and observe all day, not crawling very much at all. Other times he would become super active and wouldn't slow down!

One day, after a long day trip, we returned home, to find Gusto crawling like crazy inside the screened cage I had made, to keep him safe. I gave him his sugar water and he drank for an hour. I then let him crawl around for a while and put him to bed, in his familiar and safe book. As he stepped onto his little cloth bed, washed up and then went deeper into his bed to sleep, I discovered that Gusto was a girl! On the underside of the front cover of the book, she had laid nineteen light green eggs! Shield bugs usually lay eggs on the underside of a leaf, but she had to make-do and used the book cover instead!

It now made sense why she had bratty behavior and was so antcy for the few days before she laid her eggs and why she went to bed so early and exhausted the night before. (Her abdomen got a reddish color to it, with spots, before she laid the eggs.)

BUGS THAT LOVE! By Lori-Michele

A Ladybug, who had been in the house for two weeks, seemed to be Gusto's little pal. She'd sleep on the table or the side of the sugar water dish or in the same book on the paper with Gusto, who didn't mind and watched her often.

When the Ladybug started to die, Gusto walked right over to her and onto the same cloth about two inches away and just started to clean her antennae. She seemed to know what was happening to the Ladybug and wanted to keep her company.

I feared that maybe Gusto would catch the Ladybug's disease and pushed her away, but she returned later, to be next to her again.

When I went to wake up Gusto, about a week after the Ladybug died, she was half paralyzed. I slid her off a paper that she was on in the book, into my hand. Gusto struggled to move and crawl and her legs froze half up in the air. She still recognized me and struggled to crawl towards me, wanting to be herself, but couldn't.

I used to say to her each morning or when I'd just walk up to her, "There's the Gusto, baby!" and at night, "Nighty-night Gusto, you be a good girl." For months I said, before I knew she was a girl, "You be a good boy, Gusto," especially before leaving the house.

She loved to crawl up the front of my shirt, to get close to my face. And when I spoke close to her, she would crawl faster towards me. She liked to crawl on my shoulders and hang out there for a ride. She liked listening to my voice and got used to Dad's voice too and would walk over and look at him while he ate lunch. She also liked when I blew air on her wings, while I held her in my hand and she'd flutter and expand them for me, testing them out to make sure they were in working order and all ready to go.

While she died slowly, I carried her around with me. Sometimes, she'd stretch her back legs and move her belly, tilting it to one

BUGS THAT LOVE! By Lori-Michele

side. I think she desperately wanted to crawl and be herself again. She was very aware of being moved and would reach out and move her left front foot a bit, to communicate with me. I even tilted her once and she used the three legs on one side of her body to grip and prevent herself from falling off! It was as if she was saying, "Hey, I don't want to fall, I'm still here!"

Her antennae stood down and bent on the top notch, as the hours passed. I placed her into her favorite book at night, so she would feel there was shelter over her and not be afraid when I turned out the light. I told her I loved her and I pretended all was the same, at it had always been. I told her "It's bedtime Gusto, nighty-night, be a good girl, you are a good girl."

When I checked on her the next morning, she was still alive. I still talked to her, to give her encouragement. She was a fighter, and it was disheartening not to be able to fix her. Her mind stood sharp, but her body just gave out and she did not want to go.

All of us have a time limit in life and that is the saddest part of all... the end always comes.

I put her unfertile eggs in the box, alongside her. God rest her little soul.

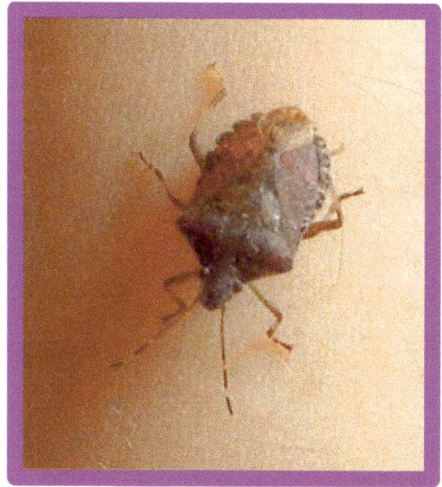

Gusto

ABOUT THE AUTHOR

Lori-Michele……has had an interesting life, to say the least. Always having compassion for all living things, when she was just three years old, she boldly use to walk up to and pet 'daddy long-legs' spiders on the back! They would sit still and enjoy the stroking, somehow knowing that she wasn't going to harm them. Although she wouldn't do that today as an adult, she embraced the outside world of nature and found everything fascinating when just a child and still does today!

She accomplished many milestones in her younger years. The first being, at the age of only 7 years old, as she won the prestigious Corn Hill Arts Festival, in Rochester, New York, with over 500 competing artists that year. She had a large exhibit of all her mixed media artwork displayed, as she expressed her feelings through her art, of what it meant to be a child of divorce.

Years later, with a perfect 4.0 GPA, she graduated from high school at 15 years old, after studying and taking the California High School Proficiency Examination. This test is meant to be so difficult that less than 5% of the students, who take the examination, pass.

For several years, she took the knowledge that she gained from an English professor who tutored her in the 10th grade and helped with her father's writing career, editing his stories for magazines and coming up with catchy titles, that would appeal to the editors and readers.

Then her life suddenly took a turn for the unexpected worse, when she was diagnosed with a rare, life-threatening (and believed to be) genetic disease, while she was only in her 20's.

After the delicate and dangerous surgery and years of long-suffering recovery, she concentrated on her first love of singing and music. She recorded 3 CD's of pop, ballads and holiday music and performed some concerts, in which she received a great and welcoming response.

During this time, she became involved in the great discovery and learning experience for nine years, coming to know and understand all the facets and emotions of the Western Conifer Seed Bug, and also, the Shield bug.

Having now completed her first book, *Bugs That Love!*, to share her experiences and to teach others all about these fascinating creatures, more is yet to come in the future from Lori-Michele.

Please visit her book website at www.bugsthatlove.com
And her music website at www.lori-michele.com

Lori-Michele is receptive to school visits, lectures, telecommunicating, as well as being a guest for radio, podcasts or TV, to further share her knowledge of these special bugs. Please use the contact page on the website.

Lori-Michele while working on this book!

Lori-Michele happily looking at pet bug.

Lori-Michele with Tina resting on her shoulder.

Lori-Michele

That's all! The End!